BEYOND THE CELEBRATION

BEYOND THE CELEBRATION

The Essential Guide to Creating a Marriage of Mutual Respect, Lasting Love, Joy, Hilarity and Great Sex

JERRY MCCOLGIN
LOU RODRIGUEZ

Beyond the Celebration – The Essential Guide to Creating a Marriage of Mutual Respect, Lasting Love, Joy, Hilarity and Great Sex © 2020 by Jerry McColgin and Lout Rodriguez. All rights reserved.

Printed in the United States of America

Published by Author Academy Elite
PO Box 43, Powell, OH 43035
www.AuthorAcademyElite.com

Scripture quotations marked NLT are taken from the Holy Bible, New Living Translation, copyright 1996, 2004. Used by permission of Tyndale House Publishers, Inc., Wheaton, Illinois 60189. All rights reserved.

Scripture quotations marked NIV are taken from the Holy Bible, New International Version. Copyright 1973, 1978, 1984 International Bible Society. Used by permission of Zondervan Bible Publishers. All rights reserved worldwide.

Identifiers:
Library of Congress Control Number: 2019921076
ISBN: 978-1-64746-095-2 (paperback)
ISBN: 978-1-64746-096-9 (hardback)
ISBN: 978-1-64746-097-6 (ebook)

All rights reserved. This book contains material protected under International and Federal Copyright Laws and Treaties. No part of this publication may be reproduced or transmitted in any form or by any means, electronic or mechanical, including photocopy, recording or any information storage and retrieval system without permission in writing from the authors.

Dedication

To our wives, for allowing us to create and live out our own shocking marriages.

CONTENTS

INTRODUCTION:
THERE'S MORE TO IT THAN PLANNING A WEDDING?   IX

PART I:
WHAT ARE YOU GETTING INTO?

CHAPTER 1: GOD'S DESIGN FOR MARRIAGE -
RESPECT THE INVENTOR   3

CHAPTER 2: BECOMING ONE FLESH -
IT TAKES MORE THAN SEX   26

CHAPTER 3: BUT WAIT, WHAT IF…?
HONESTLY, I HAVE QUESTIONS   46

PART II:
THINGS TO LEARN BEFORE THE WEDDING

CHAPTER 4: MANAGING EXPECTATIONS -
    YOU LIKE TO WHAT?   69

CHAPTER 5: MERGING LIVES -
    LEARN THE WORD "OURS"   91

PART III:
TIPS TO SUSTAINING A SHOCKING MARRIAGE

CHAPTER 6: INTIMACY -
    START HOT, STAY HOT   111

CHAPTER 7: SAFEGUARDING YOUR MARRIAGE -
    GUARDRAILS AREN'T JUST FOR HIGHWAYS   140

CHAPTER 8: EFFECTIVE COMMUNICATION -
    YOUR GREATEST TOOL   162

AFTERWORD   181

ABOUT THE AUTHORS   183

INTRODUCTION
THERE'S MORE TO IT THAN PLANNING A WEDDING?

So, you are planning to get married. Congratulations! This will be one of the most intense yet exciting seasons of your life. Dates to nail down, decisions to make, people to coordinate with—it can all be quite overwhelming. Odds are you will spend more time and money planning for this single day than any other event in your lifetime. There are plenty of resources available for planning your wedding. From fairs, expos, and magazines to wedding planners and consultants, there are numerous sources of advice and assistance to guide you through the process. A search on Amazon for "Planning a Wedding" will provide you with more than ten thousand books on this topic alone.

A search on Pinterest will provide you with thousands of ideas on themes and decorations. Every couple wants their wedding to be unique and memorable. In 2013, Napster founder Sean Parker shelled out ten million dollars for his enchanted wedding among the towering redwoods of California's Big Sur. Each of the 364 guests were given a *Lord of the Rings*-inspired costume, each made by the film's actual costume designer, to wear to the wedding. Fairy lights, petals, and garlands were strewn everywhere to recreate the elven kingdom of Rivendell, and the reception area even had fur-pelted seats and beds[1].

The average cost of a wedding in the USA for 2018 was just over thirty thousand dollars, *excluding* the honeymoon, and took on average thirteen months to plan. There were over forty-seven thousand marriages that year, which equates to $1.6 billion spent[2]. The wedding industry is a big business!

If it were up to this author (Jerry), I would change everything up. I would have people marry in a simple ceremony with only the closest family and friends to serve as witnesses. Invest in a great honeymoon so you can really get to know your spouse on an intimate level. Then throw a reception five years later to celebrate the marriage itself. Have the dinner, the dancing, and the huge party then. This could be repeated every ten years or so as desired. That would shift the emphasis from celebrating a promise to recognizing and honoring marital success. But then again, that's easy for me to say. I have two married sons and no married daughters!

The reality is that the amount you invest in your ceremony is no indicator of how successful your marriage will be. Before long you and your fiancé will stand face to face in front of your friends and family. You will look into each other's eyes and recite vows to one another. In front of God and everyone you will make promises to stand by one another for the rest of your lives. You will promise to love and support one another both in great times and in tough ones. You will verbally express your sincere intent to put your spouse's needs before your own. At that point you will be pronounced as husband and wife and begin your life together.

For many couples these vows begin to fade as quickly as a New Year's Eve resolution. It's not that there is no good intent, but rather there are no tangible action plans in place to ensure success. Just as a resolution to lose weight will fail

---

[1] Bestlifeonline.com Oct 31, 2018
[2] Business Insider August 26, 2018

if you don't incorporate diet and exercise into your lifestyle, marriage vows will fall short without focus and intention to maintain them. Returning from the honeymoon is not the time to begin figuring out "how" you intend to honor your wedding vows. Ideally that time is now.

Marital success doesn't simply happen; it takes work. Unfortunately, many couples enter into marriage completely unprepared in terms of knowing what to expect and how best to proceed. Conduct an Amazon search on "preparing for marriage" and you will only scratch the surface of all the resources available for planning a wedding. *Beyond the Celebration* is designed to help you plan for a lasting and mutually-satisfying marriage. In it you will learn about God's design for marriage and actionable steps you can take to ensure your marriage becomes all it was intended to be. Incorporating this into your preparation will help guarantee the investment you make in your wedding day (no matter the scope) is merely the beginning and not the pinnacle of your marriage.

You may not have many (or any) good role models for marriage in your life. Perhaps your parents are divorced, or the marriages you are familiar with seem tired, merely going through the motions. It doesn't have to be that way. With some attention and effort, you can create a marriage that gets better over time where laughter is more common than arguments and holding hands more prevalent than hurt feelings. We will show you how to put the steps in place to achieve that type of long-lasting, mutually-fulfilling marriage. Oh, and yeah, we'll talk about how to have great sex too!

Premarital counseling is important. Lou (one of the authors) has performed nearly a hundred weddings. He typically requires a minimum of six premarital sessions with a couple. In one of his first weddings, the couple was very anxious to get the sessions over with. Lou wondered if they were "performing" in order to please him. In fact, it seemed as if the groom had been coached on what to say. They completed the prescribed sessions and went through with the ceremony. Within a short time it was discovered one of them had been unfaithful, and the other slammed the door on any possible reconciliation. Divorce papers were quickly filed. In hindsight it is clear this couple was not really invested in the premarital counseling or planning laid out for them. Lou shares this with couples now to explain the importance of premarital counseling and preparation. It's more than a matter of checking off a to-do list. It's about preparing the heart.

This book can be used in addition to or as an integral part of your premarital counseling. Either way, work through this book together with your fiancé. Discuss the topics and answer the questions as a couple. Don't worry if some of the topics cause some heated discussion. That is perfectly natural. It is so much better to learn as much as you can about each other before the wedding so you can plan a realistic future together.

Our prayer is that this book will bless you, both as individuals and as a couple, and that you will enact plans to ensure a marriage that fulfills you both for the rest of your lives.

PART 1
WHAT ARE YOU GETTING INTO?

CHAPTER 1
GOD'S DESIGN FOR MARRIAGE - *RESPECT THE INVENTOR*

While your mind may be consumed by the dozens if not hundreds of decisions you need to make when planning your wedding, it is important you also look ahead to the marriage you will be living in for the rest of your life. To get you started in this line of thinking, ask yourself the following question: "In your mind, what does it mean to be married, and why does it interest you?" Authors Jerry and Lou have asked a lot of couples this very question during pre-marital counseling and have gotten a wide variety of answers, including, "I want to be in a committed relationship with the person I most love"; "I want to formalize our relationship so we can start a family together"; and "It just seems like the natural next step for us." Notice these answers focus more on the motivation for marrying than the actual institution of marriage. In this chapter we will help you to understand what God's intentions for marriage are and how those may be different from what our culture portrays as marriage.

Can you imagine accepting a job offer without a job description? Imagine how uncomfortable it would be to join a church only to find out later you fundamentally disagree with their beliefs. You probably wouldn't even volunteer for an organization unless you knew the expectations from a time and investment standpoint. The bottom line is most people wouldn't enter into a serious commitment without knowing what would be expected of them in return. So, why is it so many couples enter into marriage without considering the obligations and ramifications?

Marriage is one of the most important commitments you will ever voluntarily enter into. If you and your partner are Christ-followers, it makes sense you would want to know what God's design for marriage looks like in order to create a relationship that honors Him. In this chapter we will look at marriage from God's perspective and delve into the concept of covenant. None of this should intimidate you but rather should excite you about entering into a divine relationship unlike any other.

Defining Marriage from a Cultural Perspective

Before we get into God's specific design and intent for marriage, it is important to acknowledge that cultures around the world have strayed from the concept.

Dictionary.com provides the following definition for marriage:

noun

> 1. (broadly) any of the diverse forms of interpersonal union established in various parts of the world to form a familial bond that is recognized legally, religiously, or socially, granting the participating partners mutual conjugal rights and responsibilities and including, for example, opposite-sex marriage, same-sex marriage, plural marriage, and arranged marriage…

Though a broad definition, this is not all-inclusive. For example, in Bali you can legally marry your pet[3]. France is the leading country in necrogamy, the marrying of living people to those that have died[4]. In Canada, a service called "Marry Yourself Vancouver" launched in 2015. This unique organization offers consulting services and wedding photography for those who want to pursue sologamy, the act of marrying oneself[5]. It would appear from a global, secular standpoint that marriage can mean just about anything.

These are all interesting and diverse perspectives on marriage. The one thing they have in common is the legal bond formed. Beyond that they each, to differing degrees, attempt to incorporate the contemporary and cultural elements reflected in marriage. Clearly the definition of marriage has changed over the last century, and it's safe to assume it will continue to evolve in the future, continually reflecting current culture.

In many aspects of our world, change is beneficial. The advances in technology and medicine have clearly improved the quality and duration of life people enjoy today. But all change is not necessarily good. God's word is an example of timeless advice and direction applicable to our lives today exactly as it has been applied for centuries. Let's take a look at what the Bible says about marriage.

Defining Marriage from God's Perspective

Marriage is mentioned in the book of Genesis, the first book of the Bible written to describe the origins of our world. Let's look at God's design a little closer. The institution of marriage has been around since the beginning of human history. In the Bible, we first hear of it in Genesis, chapter two. For the first five days of creation, God created the heavens, the earth, the seas, the sun, the moon, and all the animals that populate the

---

[3] "How to Marry Your Pet" Wysaski, pleatedjeans.com June 2010
[4] "In France its legal to marry a corpse" Ripleys.com April 15, 2018
[5] "Why I married myself" Cosmopolitan December 20, 2016

earth. At the end of each day, He looked back and said, "It was good…" On the sixth day He made man (Adam), and to this He replied, "It is very good." He immediately put Adam in charge of everything in the Garden of Eden.

However, in verse 18 we see the following: Then the Lord God said, "It is not good for the man to be alone. I will make a helper who is just right for him" (Genesis 2:18 NLT).

This is the first time in human history God noted something wasn't *good*. It's important to note here God didn't make a mistake or realize he had overlooked something. He was not responding to Adam complaining of loneliness and begging for relief. This was simply God acknowledging he had designed Adam to be in relationship with other humans and specifically to have a lifelong partner with whom he could be in relationship and populate the earth. The chapter continues on as follows:

> …But still there was no helper just right for him. So the Lord God caused the man to fall into a deep sleep. While the man slept, the Lord God took out one of the man's ribs and closed up the opening. Then the Lord God made a woman from the rib, and he brought her to the man. "At last!" the man exclaimed. "This one is bone from my bone, and flesh from my flesh! She will be called 'woman,' because she was taken from 'man.'" This explains why a man leaves his father and mother and is joined to his wife, and the two are united into one.
>
> —Genesis 2:20-24 NLT

Verse 24 is a fascinating verse, or at least it is fascinating that it is located within this passage in Genesis. Adam had no (earthly) father or mother to leave; he was a created being. Genesis was not written in "real time" but rather was revealed to Moses at a much later date when it was captured for future generations to read. It is clear God had a plan for marriage from the moment he created Eve.

God created marriage, and His original intentions should be honored. While He filed no patent or copyright for the concept, He should be credited and respected for His design. Relationships and unions deviating from God's original design should be honored and legally protected within our society, but it is an infringement on Him to call them marriage. While our culture views marriage as a legal contract, God considers it to be something much more. He considers it a covenant between a man, a woman, and Himself.

It is clear from this passage that God's design is for one man to join with one woman in a unique, lifelong relationship where the two independent entities merge together into one flesh. There is no other relationship described as one flesh in the Bible—not between siblings, parent and child, friends, business partners, or any other combination of people.

God's Design Conflicts with Our Culture

Not every step of the relationship-forming process is called out in the Bible. The only specific direction is that one man will join one woman in a marriage covenant, and the two will become one flesh and remain together for their lifetime. The following shows a way that a relationship compatible with God's design could form.

Compatible with God's Design

- Casually date prospective partners to gauge mutual interest and basic compatibility.
- Spend time together to truly know one another and grow in relationship.
- Fall in love over time.
- Pray for direction, discernment, and blessings.
- Become engaged.
- Enter into a covenant relationship through a wedding ceremony.

- Honeymoon alone with your spouse to consummate the relationship and begin the process of becoming one flesh.
- Begin a new life sharing everything.

This process supports the scriptures we are given and is a practical methodology for creating a growing relationship leading to marriage. This might happen quickly, or it might drag out for years. It may start and stop many times with different people, but it is compatible with the design for marriage that God laid out for us.

In our culture today, movies, television shows, relationship websites, and phone apps all suggest a much different way to find a spouse. People are encouraged to treat relationships as if they are in a funnel. You start with many at the top, sift out the ones that aren't good, and end up with one at the bottom. It could be summarized as follows:

Cultural Way

- Be sexually active with multiple partners to understand your own sexual preferences and needs.
- Identify and become exclusive with a partner that is of high physical and emotional interest.
- Live together for a period of time to ensure both sexual and social compatibility.
- Have children (often times).
- Debate the pros and cons of getting married.
- Enter into a long engagement.
- Host a wedding focused on celebration.
- Reward yourself with a post-wedding vacation.
- Recover from the effort and return to pre-wedding life.

It is interesting to note that sexual incompatibility often surfaces only when an individual compares a given partner to past partners. By following God's design, you will find you are very compatible with the only other person you have sex with. Without comparing past techniques and preferences you have come to experience, you will learn to love your spouse and come to enjoy sex in a mutually satisfying manner. Sexual incompatibility is a direct result of the fallen world in which we live.

Covenant Relationships

As you prepare to enter into marriage, it is critical to understand you will be forging a relationship unlike any other you've ever had. Not only will it be different from your family and friends, but it will be different than the relationship you currently have with your partner. Up until now, you've merely been dating. Hopefully you have abstained from sexual relations to this point, but even if you have not, things will change once you are married. Ideally, on your wedding day you will enter into a new covenant relationship that includes not only your partner but God Himself. His supernatural presence will form you into one flesh with your partner over time.

It is these very two concepts, covenant and one flesh, that make a Godly marriage unique among all relationships. The remainder of this chapter will further explain the concept of covenant. The following chapter will focus on the concept of one flesh.

What is a covenant relationship? What does it mean to be in one?

The Merriam-Webster dictionary defines a covenant as "a usually formal, solemn, and binding agreement." Clearly this definition would suggest a covenant is a serious agreement, more binding than a promise or even a contract. From a Biblical standpoint scripture defines covenant as a God-inspired, solemn and binding relationship meant to last a lifetime. Before we look specifically at marriage, let's look at some other Biblical covenants to get a sense of their significance and importance.

The Old Testament depicts several covenants God made with His people. One of the earliest covenants comes from a story you are probably familiar with from childhood, the Noahic Covenant. We see in Genesis that God became so disgusted with the depravity and sinful nature of people that he sent a flood to wipe out the bulk of His creation. He chose one man, Noah, along with his family to be spared.

God gave Noah very explicit instructions on how to build an ark, and Noah did so in a spirit of obedience. The rain began and continued for forty days and forty nights, flooding the whole earth and destroying everything. As the waters finally receded, the Ark ended up on the side of a mountain. The only survivors were Noah, his family, and the animals he took with him. Once everyone vacated the ark, God made a promise (covenant) with Noah and his family.

> "Yes, I am confirming my covenant with you…Never again will a flood destroy the earth." Then God said, "I am giving you a sign of my covenant with you and with all living creatures, for all generations to come. I have placed my rainbow in the clouds. It is the sign of my covenant with you and with all the earth. When I send clouds over the earth, the rainbow will appear in the clouds, and I will remember my covenant with you and with all living creatures. Never again will the floodwaters destroy all life."
>
> —Genesis 9:11-15 NLT

You can see how this covenant clearly fits the definition given above. God initiated this solemn and binding covenant and made it not only with Noah and his family but with all living creatures on the Earth. It wasn't a limited-time agreement, nor was it to last merely for the duration of Noah's life. God made this covenant for all generations to come. We still live under this covenant today.

The other important item to note is the sign of the covenant. Though verse 15 states "I will remember my covenant between me and you…" it is not implying God might forget about it otherwise. The rainbow was not created to remind God but rather to remind us that this covenant is still in place today.

The second covenant God initiated was with Abraham (Abrahamic Covenant) where he promised a future blessing for His chosen people.

> "This is my covenant with you: I will make you the father of a multitude of nations!"
>
> —Genesis 17:4 NLT

> "I will confirm my covenant with you and your descendants after you, from generation to generation. This is the everlasting covenant: I will always be your God and the God of your descendants after you. And I will give the entire land of Canaan, where you now live as a foreigner, to you and your descendants. It will be their possession forever, and I will be their God."
>
> —Genesis 17:7-8 NLT

All men of a certain age (covered under this covenant) were required to be circumcised as a sign.

A third, significant covenant was made between God and Moses. As you may recall, the Israelites were held as slaves in the burgeoning country of Egypt. After several hundred years in captivity, the Lord heard the captives' pleas and sent Moses to free them. This is a fascinating story in the book of Exodus involving many miraculous signs from God that were used to finally convince Pharaoh to let the Israelites go. Once free from Egypt, they set up camp, and Moses climbed a mountain to hear further instructions from God. It was at this time that God made the following covenant with Moses.

> "Now if you will obey me and keep my covenant, you will be my own special treasure from among all the peoples on earth; for all the earth belongs to me…"
>
> —Exodus 19:5 NLT

We see here the formation of what is typically called the Old Covenant. In this covenant the Israelites were set apart as God's chosen people. In the following months God laid out the ways in which this nation could access God and how, through a series of blood sacrifices and the intercession of priests and high priests, they could be cleansed of their sins.

As with the previous covenants, for this Mosaic covenant God provided the ten commandments as a sign.

In each of these examples we see the aforementioned terms of covenant were met.

- God-inspired
- Solemn and binding
- Meant to last a lifetime (or longer)

When we fast-forward a few hundred years, we see the prophet Malachi speaking to the Israelites. He was sent by God to address the lax religious and social behavior that had become prevalent in their culture. As a part of his rebuke we see the following marriage-specific instruction.

> Another thing you do: You flood the Lord's altar with tears. You weep and wail because he no longer looks with favor on your offerings or accepts them with pleasure from your hands. You ask, "Why?" It is because the Lord is the witness between you and the wife of your youth. You have been unfaithful to her, though she is your partner, the wife of your marriage covenant.
>
> —Malachi 2:13-14 NIV

While we don't have the same level of detail regarding this covenant, we can clearly see marriage is considered to be a covenant in God's eyes.

Your Marriage Covenant

When you enter into marriage as believers, you enter into a binding, life-long, intimate covenant with both God and your spouse. It is a three-way relationship as illustrated below.

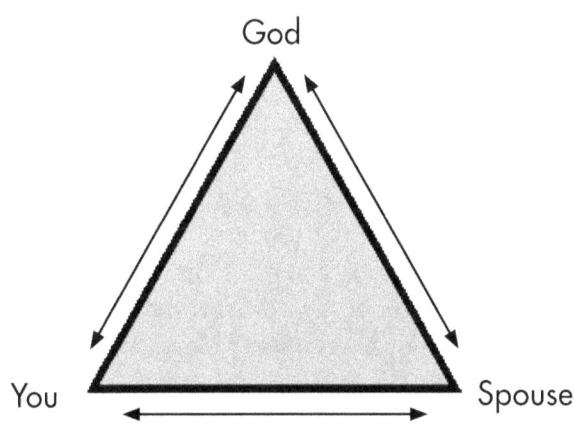

Each leg of this relationship triangle is essential from a covenant perspective. The relationship you have with your spouse is predicated on the fact that you each have a solid relationship with God. When this takes place, you have invited God to be an active part of your marriage. Through his Holy Spirit he will direct you, guide you, inspire you, and comfort you. It is critical that you and your spouse recognize God as an integral part of your marriage. He should be included when you make big decisions, when you seek counsel, and when you find yourselves in dispute. His intent is not to be a "silent partner" but rather a very active member of your covenant relationship. We see the purpose of God in our marriages in the following passage.

> Two people are better off than one, for they can help each other succeed. If one person falls, the other can reach out and help. But someone who falls alone is in real trouble. Likewise, two people lying close together can keep each other warm. But how can one be warm alone? A person

standing alone can be attacked and defeated, but two can stand back-to-back and conquer. Three are even better, for a triple-braided cord is not easily broken.

—Ecclesiastes 4:9-12 NLT

This passage is frequently used in wedding ceremonies. It depicts the power and strength God provides in a marriage relationship. When you enter into a covenant relationship with God and your spouse, you have that third strand that will keep you together and strong.

Typically, rings are exchanged during the wedding ceremony. These rings serve the same purpose in our lives as the rainbow. They are a tangible, constant reminder of the covenant relationship we are under. You don't only wear your ring when you are with your spouse. You wear it in all situations. It serves both to remind you of your commitment to your spouse and to God while you are apart as well as to let others know you are in a sacred relationship with another.

Dennis Rainey, a well-known Christian family life speaker, writes the following on the topic of marriage:

> For the past two years I have had a growing concern that the Christian community has passively watched the "dumbing down" of the marriage covenant. Marriage has become little more than an upgraded social contract between two people—not a holy covenant between a man and a woman and their God for a lifetime. In the Old Testament days, a covenant was solemn and binding. When two people entered into a covenant with one another, a goat or lamb would be slain, and its carcass would be cut in half. With the two halves separated and lying on the ground, the two people who had formed the covenant would solemnize their promise by walking between the two halves saying, "May God do so to me [cut me in half] if I ever break this covenant with you and God!" You get

the feeling that a covenant in those days had just a little more substance than today[6].

Renowned Christian minister and author Jack Hayford has similar words:

> The covenant of marriage is the single most important human bond that holds all of God's work on the planet together. It is no small wonder that the Lord is passionate about the sanctity of marriage and the stability of the home. This covenant of marriage is based on the covenant God has made with us. It is in the power of His promise to her mankind that our personal covenant of marriage can be kept against the forces that would destroy homes and ruin lives[7].

While most couples are unaware of this fact, many of our wedding traditions stem back to covenant ceremonies from the Bible. As was mentioned in the Dennis Rainey excerpt, it was customary for two parties entering into a covenant agreement to sacrifice an animal, cut it in two, and walk between the two halves of the carcass.

We still see other ancient traditions today:

- The bride's family is seated on one side of the church, and the groom's sits on the other.
- The bride enters the church down the center aisle, symbolizing the cutting of the blood covenant.
- The white runner down the center aisle represents holy ground where two lives are joined as one by God.
- Earthly marriages are a picture of Christ's union with the church. Christ is the groom and will come back to meet his

---

[6] "The Covenant of Marriage" Rainey
[7] Hayford, J. W. The Spirit-Filled Family: Holy Wisdom to Build Happy Homes. Nashville: Thomas Nelson

- bride. The groom entering first represents Him waiting for His bride.
- The wedding veil is a representation of the temple veil. When Christ died on the cross, the temple veil was torn in two, giving believers direct access to God for the first time. When the veil is lifted in a wedding ceremony, the bride and groom are given full access to one another.
- At the end of the ceremony, the minister will typically pronounce the couple as husband and wife. This moment establishes the precise beginning of their covenant with God.

There are many more examples like those shown above, including the holding of right hands, the exchanging of rings, the giving of the bride by her father, etc. The point is that after all these years traditional Christian weddings are relying on customs from thousands of years ago.

One of the most important parts of the covenant ceremony is the moment the couple recites their wedding vows to one another. A vow is a solemn promise, not a statement of "I'll try my hardest." I've never been to a wedding and heard a couple list their marriage goals or their best intentions. You will typically hear some version of the following during a Christian wedding:

- You take ____ to be your lawfully wedded spouse, pledging before God and these witnesses to be ever faithful, devoted. and true…
- …in sickness and in health…
- …for richer or poorer…
- …for better or worse…
- …until death do us part.

These aren't fuzzy, conditional agreements but rather are solemn promises a couple chooses to make to each other before God.

While for some couples these vows may be a mere formality, I believe most couples have the best of intentions to honor them. I encourage you as you plan for your wedding to spend some significant time in prayer and meditation over the vows you will say. These are not statements made in passing. They are promises made before the Lord and should be taken very seriously. Pray that God will give you the strength to honor these vows even when things get tough. That is a tremendous way to ensure you, your spouse, and God are all on the same page from the start.

The sad fact is that the importance of the aforementioned verse in Ecclesiastes (…*let no one split apart what God has joined together.*) seems to have been lost in our culture. Based on the divorce rate in our culture, you'd think many wedding ceremonies might sound more like the following:

> "… As of today, I'll agree to make efforts to stay married to you as long as things are good, I stay happy, and you continue to satisfy my ongoing needs. However, if things get tough, or if I outgrow you or decide I've fallen out of love, I reserve the right to move on in pursuit of my own ultimate happiness. I hope things work out, but if they don't, they don't."

We seem to have lost the importance, even the meaning of the word "vow." When you make a vow, you are agreeing to behave in a certain manner for a designated period of time. In the case of marriage, that timeframe would extend until the death of either you or your partner.

Are All Marriages Covenants?

Historically, the only way a covenant could be nullified was if it were replaced with a new covenant. The greatest example of this can be seen In the Bible. The Old Covenant God had with His chosen people was ultimately replaced (or fulfilled) by the New Covenant when Jesus died on the cross and was resurrected from the dead. So, today we no longer live under the governance of the Old Covenant but rather under the New.

It's important then that we consider marriage in light of this New Covenant. What did Jesus say about marriage?

Lest you think marriage covenants are strictly an Old Testament concept, we read in the book of Mark that Jesus was speaking to his disciples about marriage. He reiterates the passage from Genesis but expands on it a bit.

"But 'God made them male and female' from the beginning of creation. 'This explains why a man leaves his father and mother and is joined to his wife, and the two are united into one.' Since they are no longer two but one, let no one split apart what God has joined together" (Mark 10:6-9 NLT).

Jesus adds the crucial line asserting no one should split apart a couple God has brought together. This further supports the notion of marriage being a sacred covenant meant to last a lifetime. Whereas the New Covenant replaced (or fulfilled) the Old Covenant in the Bible, it is clear the design and intent for marriage was to be unchanged.

In this same setting, a group of Pharisees discoursed with Jesus. They tried to trap him by asking him if a man could divorce his wife for any reason.

Jesus replied, "Moses permitted divorce only as a concession to your hard hearts, but it was not what God had originally intended. And I tell you this, whoever divorces his wife and marries someone else commits adultery—unless his wife has been unfaithful" (Matthew 19:8-9 NLT).

In Old Testament times women were treated like property. A covenant of marriage was much like a contract of ownership. Women were "given" in marriage to secure a treaty between two nations or even neighboring cities. The Old Testament is filled with stories of fathers giving their daughters in marriage as a part of a negotiated deal. When the marriage relationship was no longer of value to the man, he could divorce his wife and send her away. In this passage Jesus explains how that practice was already a departure from God's original plan.

Today, just as women personally choose to accept and follow Jesus as their Lord and Savior, they choose who they want to marry. A Christ-following woman makes this choice not out of a sense of obligation but rather through a longing and a desire to enter into a covenant relationship with a man she believes God has brought into her life. It is through this willingness and calling that God joins two people together into marriage.

Jesus said, "Let no one split apart what God has joined together…" It is important to note here that God does *not* join all couples together. Free will allows you to make decisions in your life outside of God's will. You can be legally and contractually married at the courthouse by a judge or on a ship by a captain. You can even be married by an atheist friend who got his credentials online a week before the ceremony. You may have all the rights of a married person, but that does not put you into a covenant relationship with your spouse and with God. Likewise, you can have a beautiful, formal wedding in a spectacular cathedral, but without making a full, heartfelt commitment to be in a covenant relationship with God, you are not joined together through Him. It's not about who marries you or where the ceremony takes place. It is about the conscious decision you and your spouse enter into with and before God.

It's ironic how this notion has been distorted through our culture. Couples get married in a church by a pastor, surrounded by friends and families serving as witnesses. They make promises, committing their relationship to God as they enter into this covenant. Then when things go south, they privately enter into a courtroom with lawyers and judges as they seek divorce. What God has joined together they ask man to separate. Once the divorce is finalized, the individuals often find themselves celebrating their newfound "freedom" on social media or with their friends.

Scripture shows us that a given covenant can be replaced with a new covenant. But it is important to remember that God is a part of a marriage covenant. He gives us an out for infidelity, but otherwise He expects us to work through trials and issues. Even in the case of infidelity, if the offending partner comes forward with a truly repentant heart, seeking forgiveness, the other can choose to show grace and begin work on restoring the marriage.

To recap, God-designed marriage is a covenant. A covenant is a binding, sacred commitment that includes you, your spouse, and God. It is unlike any other relationship you will be in. There is comfort and security in being in a covenant, but there are responsibilities as well. Just as we know God won't wipe out the world again with a flood, you can know your marriage is protected as long as you abide by the commitments made during your wedding. This is not something to be feared; this is a wonderful arrangement you are about to enter into. Take your covenant vows seriously, then rest in the assurance that your marriage is in God's hands.

Jerry's Story

I met Tara in junior high. We had several friends in common and found ourselves running in the same group in many social situations. I remember having a distant crush on Tara for a couple of years, but I was too afraid to talk to her one-on-one. In high school I began dating other girls but kept my eye on Tara. By the time I was a junior, I worked up the nerve to ask Tara out, and she agreed. I took her out for some fast food, then a movie. As I recall, we had a great time with lots of laughter and conversation. When I took her home, I walked her to the door and gave her a quick kiss. As I was walking back to my car, my mind was filled with foreknowledge: "I'm going to marry that girl." It was as clear a voice or thought as I'd ever had, and I knew it would come true.

Interestingly, Tara did not get any such revelation, and that posed some challenges for me. I persisted in asking her out for more dates. She would concede sometimes and refuse others. When we were together, we would have a great time. But when I saw her at school between dates, she would intentionally avoid me. She had no interest in growing close to me and did not want to be in any type of serious relationship at such a young age. At one point she had a mutual friend tell me I should back off because she had no interest in ever being more than friends with me. I vividly remember calling her only to hear that those were in fact her sentiments. She asked me politely to give her space. You can imagine my conundrum. Why would I back off from my future wife and passively watch her date other guys?

I was more serious about some of the girls I dated before Tara than others, but any time I got even the whiff that something might be wrong, I bailed out of the relationship. I didn't want the pain or frustration of heartbreak. So, when I uttered the following words to Tara, "Do you mind if I keep trying to win you over?" I was as shocked as she must have been. I asked her out for the following weekend and was turned down due to some conflict she had. Without missing a beat, I invited her for the weekend after and heard the same rejection for a different reason. She finally ran out of excuses and agreed to go on a date with me about a month later. From her perspective, she was never "anti-Jerry." She simply was not ready to get tied down in a serious relationship. She certainly couldn't understand or appreciate my persistence.

Over the next few years I won her over, and our relationship blossomed. We married at a young age; I was twenty-one, and she was just twenty. I knew I loved her and wanted to be with her full time. I was in my junior year at Purdue University. My parents were putting me through college, so I had no financial concerns. Tara, on the other hand, was putting herself through school. As a result, she worked full-time and took classes in the evening as she could afford them. During my junior year she had saved up enough to be able to move to campus at Purdue and live in the dorms. I was ecstatic. It was incredible having her so nearby, able to spend evenings and weekends together. But as she looked at her finances, it became clear she would have to leave school at the end of the year and return to work. The cost of living on campus full-time was simply prohibitive for her situation. I was devastated. I began doing some research and found that the least expensive place to live on campus was married student housing. I ran the numbers and went to my father with a request. I showed him he could pay for us both to live in the married apartments for little or no more than he was paying to house me in a dormitory. If Tara didn't have to pay the living expenses, she could work on campus and cover her tuition.

Fortunately, my dad thought the world of Tara and was a big advocate of marriage. He agreed this would make financial sense and said he would support us in this manner.

With the opportunity in sight, I immediately sought out jobs on campus so I could buy her an engagement ring. I worked on the grounds crew mowing lawns, and I worked in the large auditorium, setting up and tearing down for traveling shows and concerts. I never told Tara why I was working. I merely explained I was trying to save up some money. Late that fall I took my savings and bought her a ring. Granted, it was a small diamond—but as far as I was concerned, it was the most beautiful ring I'd ever seen. When Christmas break came around, I proposed.

We were married the next summer in a simple ceremony at my church. It was a relatively short engagement, driven by the fact that we had to be wed to live in married student housing. We went through some mandatory pre-marital counseling at the small church where I'd been raised, but neither of us felt very challenged by the process. The minister meant well, but weddings were infrequent, so this was an area he did not deal with very often.

At that point in our lives, Tara had yet to receive Christ, and my faith was minimal. We got married in a church because that was what you did back then. We had no teaching about nor grasp of the concept of a covenant relationship. In fact, I doubt I could have even defined the word *covenant*. We repeated the vows provided by the minister. We meant them (at least in the moment), but that part seemed to be a matter of routine rather than a sacred moment. We went back to Purdue my senior year as a married couple, both enrolled as full-time students.

Ours was not a typical first year of marriage. At that time, you could legally have alcohol in married student housing. Our apartment became a hangout for my beer-guzzling buddies. Tara and I saw little of each other during the week because of our conflicting class schedules, and weekends I would typically have four or five of my friends over until the wee hours. In some ways our life was more like a continuous frat party than an early marriage.

While Tara liked my friends, she was trying to set up a home for the two of us. She became agitated at the mess she would see upon rising on a Saturday or Sunday morning. She did not appreciate walking to the kitchen for coffee in her pajamas only to find a snoring buddy passed out on our couch. Without her realizing it, seeds of doubt and discontent about our marriage were being planted in her mind.

I graduated during a severe recession, and jobs were tight. Our apartment lease ended at the end of May. Without a job we had no choice but to move to my parents' house as I continued my career search. While my parents were very supportive, living under their roof provided considerable stress for both of us, but especially for Tara. From her perspective the first nine months of marriage had seemed unreal, but this transition felt even worse. She felt like we were both children playing grown-up. The seeds planted during the school year began to take root.

In the following weeks, I received a job offer from a manufacturer of automobile tires. The starting salary was well below the average offered to engineers fresh out of school. Plus the job would be in a dirty (think black rubber dust covering your shoes and clothing) factory environment with little to no growth potential in the future. There was nothing about that company that interested me, so I turned them down. Tara was desperate to get out of my parent's home and pled with me that something was better than nothing. That became a major point of contention between us.

Fortunately, I received a solid job offer in a neighboring state within a couple more weeks. I readily accepted that one, and we moved to our first non-student apartment. For both of us it finally felt like we were grown up and married. We were excited about the future and beginning our new lives together.

That dream didn't last very long. I poured myself into my new job both professionally and socially. I worked long hours and spent many evenings in the bar across the street during happy hour. In my mind, I was networking with fellow employees and creating critical relationships for my future. Meanwhile, Tara was commuting two hours every day to finish her college degree. We continued to live largely independent lives. The seeds planted in each of our minds were now growing into weeds.

In the years that followed, we relocated a couple times with my job. But each of us continued to live a selfish existence, more focused on our own interests and pleasures than serving one another. If you had looked at our marriage from an outside, objective perspective, you would say our wedding day was the peak of our relationship and that we slowly grew apart from that point on.

Five years into our marriage we had our first son. Having a child changed our lives. It was a point to bond around, but lack of sleep and frustration accompanied the joy. By the time he turned two, I felt a strong need to begin attending church. I had been raised going to Sunday school as a kid, and I felt like my son needed the same experience. After several weeks of church shopping, we found a place that was both comfortable and challenging at the same time.

Not long after finding that church, Tara accepted Christ, and I rededicated myself to the Lord shortly thereafter. It was at that point when we took our first serious look at our marriage and came to see what it represented in God's eyes. While we didn't go through a formal or public rededication ceremony, we decided to commit our marriage to the Lord. That was a huge turning point for us and our relationship. As we focused our lives on God, we found ourselves now desiring to serve one another in a more selfless manner.

Do I believe God brought the two of us together? Without a doubt in my mind. I *knew* nearly from the beginning of our relationship that Tara was the one for me. I pursued her in that knowledge, even when things were rocky in our dating life. But for the first several years of our marriage I did not treat her as the gift from God she truly was. Did God "join" us together on that hot summer day? I don't think so. While we were legally married, I believe we were joined together in covenant the moment we committed our marriage to Him. I know that it has been a wonderful and exciting experience ever since that time. I am wholeheartedly committed to my vows now. And we have had richer and poorer experiences, great times and really tough times. But I know all three of us (God, Tara, and I) expect to be in this marriage covenant until death do us part, for which I take tremendous comfort.

Summary

God created the concept of marriage as a part of His overall design. Our culture has veered far from His original intent, and we see the struggles that have resulted. You can choose to follow God's design by entering into a covenant relationship committed to last for life. Keeping God as the focus in your marriage will bring you blessings in great times and provide you with strength in tough times. As you prepare the vows you intend to share during your wedding, take time to really consider and pray through what you are committing to. Then hold yourselves accountable to the promises you make.

Discussion Questions

1. In your own words, what is God's design for marriage?

2. What makes a covenant marriage unique when compared to other marriages?

3. What are the benefits of a covenant marriage?

4. Are you and your fiancé in agreement to enter into a covenant marriage?

5. What will you do to keep God as the focus in your relationship?

CHAPTER 2
BECOMING ONE FLESH - *IT TAKES MORE THAN SEX*

I don't know about you, but when I think about the challenging concept of two humans becoming one flesh, I think of fruit trees. That's right, fruit trees. As you are probably aware, every piece of fruit, regardless of type, contains a pit or seeds in one form or another. You might assume these seeds are gathered and planted to grow new trees. That's actually not the case in many situations. Rather, a process called *grafting* is used. In this process small stems are pruned from a mature tree in the winter after the leaves have fallen. In the spring a separate, typically young tree is selected. This tree is cut off, leaving only the trunk. A knife is used to cut a notch into the trunk and peel back the bark. They whittle the bark off the stems to expose the inner part of the branch. These stems are then physically inserted into the trunk of the host tree. After only a few weeks they begin to receive nourishment and grow.

Here's the amazing part. Stems from two different types of related trees can be used. As an example, a peach branch and a plum branch (both considered stone fruits because of their large, hard pits) could both be grafted into the same trunk. Over time each would begin to grow and develop while continuing to produce their respective fruits. Each branch would be fully dependent on the trunk for nutrients and life. Though the fruits remain different, the two unique stems grow into a single, full-sized, living tree. This is quite a sight to behold—a single fruit tree bearing both yellow and purple fruit!

Let's tie the idea of grafting to the concept of a man and a woman becoming one flesh. In a believer's marriage, a man and a woman come together in covenant and become one flesh by being jointly grafted into God. While they may come to look and act more like each other over time, they are still different people, bearing unique fruit. But like the grafted fruit tree they become one flesh, sharing sustenance and life in a covenant with God himself.

This was God's original plan, for one man and one woman to be joined together in a lifelong, one-flesh, covenant relationship. This is a description unlike any other relationship mentioned in the Bible. When God said it was not good for Adam to be alone, he created Eve to be his helper. This is in no way implies Eve was inferior to Adam. Rather, Eve was created to complete Adam. While Adam was God's "perfect creation," Eve provided additional perspectives, skills, and attributes that made him better. Interestingly, the same word, *helper*, is used to describe the Lord in Hebrews 13:6: "The Lord is my helper, so I will have no fear…" It is clear based on this context that Eve was not intended to be subordinate to Adam.

We are all made in God's image, both male and female. God possesses all the characteristics traditionally associated with both men and women. God's design was (and is still) to bring a man and a woman together to create something more complete than what either person could provide on their own. It is a supernatural co-mingling of two lives.

We live in a conflicted culture. We take pride in our uniqueness, our abilities, and our self-sufficiency. With individuality being so heavily emphasized, we are taught that we can become anything or anyone we want to be. At the same time social norms that once dictated how genders were to look and behave have blurred. Today we hear that there are no real differences between men and women and that any individual can decide themselves what gender they most identify with. Many states now provide the option to not indicate a gender on a birth certificate, allowing the child to choose which sex they best identify with once they become of age. Culturally we are allowing individual preference to supersede God's original biological design.

For some the thought of becoming one flesh with another person is appalling. They perceive it as becoming codependent or giving up a part of themselves. Since the time when Adam and Eve fell prey to temptation, we have lived in a fallen world. God's original design for our lives and for marriage has been compromised as our human natures have led us astray. One need only look at the statistics regarding divorce, infidelity, cohabitation, and sex addiction to see evidence of this fact.

As believers we don't have to fall into these traps. We can choose to follow God's original design and accept his intended blessing. That sounds easy, but even for the most devout of believers it can be a challenge. Becoming one flesh with your spouse is nothing to fear. Paul called the concept a "profound mystery" (Ephesians 5:32) and went on to say that marriage is a representation of Christ and the church. Couples that have fully embraced the concept would call it a blessing.

Lou had the sacred privilege of being present in a hospital room where the husband of a one-flesh marriage of more than fifty years was in the process of passing away. It was a sad time of loss because these partners would not see each other again until she passed away. But it was a sacred time as well because the Lord was very present in that room. His wife held him, and prayers were uttered by both her and their children—not prayers of healing but prayers thanking God for being the Lord of their marriage. It was a sweet homecoming but only possible because they had embraced the one-flesh covenant truth.

The Role of Sex in Becoming One Flesh

We've talked a lot about becoming one flesh, but how exactly does that happen? There has been considerable theological debate over this concept. One common line of thinking believes it is the act of sexual intercourse that causes two individuals to become one flesh. This thinking is supported by the writings of Paul in the Bible:

> Do you not know that your bodies are members of Christ himself? Shall I then take the members of Christ and unite them with a prostitute? Never! Do you not know that he who unites himself with a prostitute is one with her in body? For it is said, "The two will become one flesh."
>
> —1 Corinthians 6:15-16

Clearly sex plays an integral role in the one flesh concept. Going back to God's original design, "Adam and his wife were both naked, and they felt no shame" (Genesis 2:25 NLT). Nudity and sex were completely natural, and there was no guilt associated with either. They were completely transparent with one another and had nothing to hide. God's original plan was that one man would come together with one woman in marriage. They would have sex, generate Godly offspring, and remain together for life. Over the course of this process, they would together become one flesh. In this idyllic scenario, it makes perfect sense that sex would be the trigger to sealing the covenant and creating one flesh. But sin entered the world when Adam and Eve fell prey to the devil's lure. At this point God's original plan was disrupted as you can see in the following scripture:

> When the woman saw that the fruit of the tree was good for food and pleasing to the eye, and also desirable for gaining wisdom, she took some and ate it. She also gave some to her husband, who was with her, and he ate it. Then

the eyes of both of them were opened, and they realized they were naked; so they sewed fig leaves together and made coverings for themselves. Then the man and his wife heard the sound of the Lord God as he was walking in the garden in the cool of the day, and they hid from the Lord God among the trees of the garden. But the Lord God called to the man, "Where are you?" He answered, "I heard you in the garden, and I was afraid because I was naked; so I hid." And he said, "Who told you that you were naked? Have you eaten from the tree that I commanded you not to eat from?" The man said, "The woman you put here with me—she gave me some fruit from the tree, and I ate it." Then the Lord God said to the woman, "What is this you have done?" The woman said, "The serpent deceived me, and I ate."

—Genesis 3:5-13 NIV

Everything changed when sin entered the world, including sex and marriage. It is safe to assume that by this point in the story Adam and Eve had engaged in sexual relations. If that were the only criteria to make them one flesh, then they would have been so when God confronted them. When Adam is asked about eating the apple, he immediately blames Eve for his indiscretion. "The woman you put here with me..." It's as if he is saying, "It's not my fault, God. You sent that woman here. She ate it first. She talked me into it. I never would have eaten it otherwise. It's all her fault." When confronted, Adam clearly wanted to distance himself from Eve to avoid receiving blame for disobeying God. It doesn't appear these two were really behaving as if they were one flesh at this point. The question is, did they become one flesh when they had sex for the first time? Or could it be that becoming one flesh is really a process that happens over time with God's blessing?

Let's again look back at God's original intent. One man would join one woman in a covenant relationship with Himself. They would consummate the relationship and never open themselves to sexual relations with another person in the future. Just as the unique and distinct branches grafted into a strong, well-rooted trunk became one tree, their ongoing, intimate relationship would become as one flesh as they spent the remainder of their lives together.

God backed up his original intent in the very design of our human bodies. From a biological standpoint, scientists have found that a part of our brain releases a hormone called oxytocin when we experience intimacy with another person. Sometimes called the "cuddle hormone," oxytocin actually creates a bond between two people. This hormone is released in a variety of instances, including when a mother breastfeeds her baby. But a significant amount of oxytocin is also generated during sex. Sex is intended to occur only within marriage; this hormone serves to bond husband and wife together in a very real sense.

You can see the role that sex was intended to have in the one flesh creation process, but how does that work in our fallen world today? A 2018 study found that US men had (on average) 7.2 sexual partners in their lifetime. Women followed close behind with 6.8. Clearly that's a departure from God's original intent.

Lou was the middle school pastor at a megachurch where he taught a series on purity and sex. He provided the following illustration for the kids one Sunday. He took a blue Lego and a red Lego and held up each in a separate hand. He put them together and held them up for the kids to see. "How many bricks do I have now?" he asked. The kids all shouted, "Two!" He agreed and pulled them apart with ease. He said this illustrated a typical, casual relationship between two people. They can come together and separate with no issues. He told the kids that this is how dating should be. Two individuals could be together as one couple, but they retained their individual identities. Come together, have some fun, see how socially compatible you might be. That was all good. If the dating came to an end, the couple could separate, but there were no long-term issues continuing the relationship as just friends.

Then he took a tube of super glue from his pocket, put a couple of drops on each brick, and then pressed them back together. He explained that this illustrated what happens when the two become sexually active. He passed the bricks around for the kids to handle. "How many bricks do we have now?" he asked again. "Two," the kids replied, clearly still seeing one red and one blue Lego. He invited them to divide them and show him two bricks. With the plastic toys being chemically welded together, no one could pull them apart. "Are there really still two Legos, or is there now just one?" he asked. After some discussion, most of the kids finally agreed that, for all practical purposes, there was now only one brick. He went on to explain that the glue had joined the two individual pieces into one piece and stated that having sex with someone does the same thing in our lives, citing the scripture from 1 Corinthians as support. He explained that this was how God intended it to be in his original design.

But he didn't leave it there. He explained that in our fallen world sex alone is not enough to keep a couple together for a lifetime. He then took the two bricks and forcibly separated them with a screwdriver. He held the two up again and reiterated the question, "Now how many bricks do we have?" The kids immediately jumped on the fact that there were two again. He concurred. He then invited the kids to look closely at each brick. Though they had in fact been separated, there were clearly fragments of the red brick on the blue one and fragments of the blue brick on the red one. He went on to explain that while these two bricks had been separated, each would carry fragments of the other brick with them forever.

To further his illustration, he then proceeded to glue the red brick to a new yellow brick and then forcibly separated these two bricks apart. As he held up each brick, he showed how the red brick now had shards of both the yellow and the blue brick permanently adhered to it. But even more interestingly, he showed the kids that if they looked closely, they could see small fragments of the blue brick on the yellow brick, even though they had never come in direct contact with each other.

At this point he told the students, "When you have sex with a person, you have sex with every person that person has had sex with." Holding up the now deformed red brick drove this point home in a very real manner.

As a final point, he demonstrated that it was now nearly impossible to unite the red brick with another brick without the use of glue. So much of the original design was missing or distorted that it would not automatically form a strong bond with a new brick as it was originally designed.

His point was clear. Each time a person takes on a sexual partner, they lose a bit of themselves and carry around a part of the other person (at least in their memory) forever. After a while it becomes harder and harder to form a meaningful, intimate relationship with another person.

It is clear what we do with our bodies sexually leaves a lasting imprint on our souls. It is easy to understand that God's intent was that this imprint should only exist with our spouse. Various studies done in the early 2000s estimate that only between three and eight percent of couples are both virgins when they get married. Clearly they can become one flesh, but what about all the others?

Consider this from a purely secular perspective. If man A and woman B had sex and became one flesh, then wouldn't every person who had sex with either of them, by definition, become one flesh with each of them? 1970's NBA star Wilt Chamberlain claimed in his autobiography to have slept with twenty thousand women. Playboy founder Hugh Hefner claims to have slept with over a thousand women. One has to assume that their "partners" were probably not monogamous and had numerous partners of their own. If each of these hookups created one flesh and each partner had an average number of additional relationships, you can see that these two men by themselves led to over one million one-flesh relationships. The only people spared from this giant "six degrees of one flesh" would be the three to eight percent of couples that were virgins when they married and remained exclusive to one partner throughout their lives.

Scripture paints a different picture. "But the person who is joined to the Lord is one spirit with him" (1 Corinthians 6:17 NLT).

This would imply that the opposite is also true: whoever is not united with the Lord is *not* one with him in spirit. Becoming one flesh is a supernatural process driven by God. If a person is not one with God in spirit, it is highly unlikely He would intervene in this manner. Happily married couples may grow to act like one another, but without being one in spirit with God, they will never truly become one flesh. All the ingredients must be in place for this one-flesh blessing to occur—one man and one woman married in a covenant relationship with God. God never intended for multiple people to be one flesh. The blessings that come from being one flesh are a gift to married couples in a covenant relationship with God.

Gaining a One Flesh Perspective

So, what does living as one flesh look like in real life? It's not that individuals are seen as "incomplete" when away from their spouse, but their words and actions do reflect something beyond themselves. If I'm at work and someone initiates a meeting during business hours, I simply look at my calendar and either accept the invitation or suggest an alternative if I have a conflict. However, if someone asks me if I'd like to do something during the evening or on a weekend, I tell them I need to first talk with my wife as she is the keeper of the family calendar. It's not that I need her permission to do something during non-work hours, but out of respect I acknowledge that family time involves more people than myself. Plus, she is much better at managing multiple people's schedules than I am, so I am playing to her giftedness as well.

Once you are married, you no longer live for merely yourself. Your actions and decisions affect another person, so they need to be considered. You will need to consciously avoid inducing pain for your spouse. You would never pick up a hammer and smash your own thumb on purpose. (I've done that accidently, so I am keenly aware of the pain and damage that causes.) With a one-flesh perspective that awareness of pain avoidance should extend beyond you to your spouse. Pain is not necessarily physical. Insensitivity can cause emotional pain as well. Think beyond your own desires and consider your partner. Comparing your spouse to another or making them the target of public jokes is an example of causing direct, unnecessary pain.

It is possible to cause indirect pain as well. Prioritizing something over your spouse is an example of this. I know of guys that went out with coworkers for a drink after work. If a guy goes and realizes he's having a good time, he might decide to stay longer than he'd originally intended. His wife expects him home at a certain time for dinner, but he comes home late. The message received is that his coworkers are more important than she is. The same could be said if a wife agreed to a girl's weekend away without first consulting her husband. These are both examples of causing indirect pain.

When people lose their one-flesh perspective, they become self-absorbed, concerned only with their own pleasure. They make concerted efforts to hide their actions from their spouse. In that case their motivation is to avoid the personal pain and conflict that would inevitably occur if they were found out. A one-flesh perspective drives a person to consider their spouse in the moment. It's not a sin to be tempted; it's only a sin to act on that temptation. I remember a few years ago people wore rubber bracelets with *WWJD* printed on them, an acronym for "What Would Jesus Do?" These were to serve as a reminder that when we make choices, we should consider this question. Along these same lines, if I were to market a line of similar bracelets, they would read *WWMST* (What Would My Spouse Think). This comes naturally to people with a one-flesh perspective, but it's one of the first things to go when the relationship begins to deteriorate.

There is synergy in a one-flesh relationship. According to the concept of synergy, two people working effectively together produce results greater than the two combined could do on their own. You may have heard it described as "one plus one equals three." There's tremendous truth in that. A husband and wife united and working toward the same goals will surpass most other individuals working alone. It's important to note here that Satan will work hard to disrupt this effectiveness. If he can change the perspective from one flesh back to individualism, he goes a long way toward this end. When we begin making decisions and plans based strictly on our own desires, a wedge is placed in our relationships.

I don't know if you've ever split wood using a wedge. It's quite simple but fascinating to watch. A wedge is a heavy piece of solid steel shaped like a triangle. The sharp end is placed down on the log, and the blunt, wide end is struck with a sledgehammer. At first it takes considerable effort to get the wedge into the wood, but after repeated striking it finds itself driven into the log. With each blow of the sledge the wedge drives itself deeper into the log, and the log begins to divide into two parts. Interestingly, the wood splits very slowly at first. But at some point the wedge exerts such pressure inside the log that a single blow from the hammer causes the log to practically fly into two pieces.

> The one flesh in marriage is not just a physical phenomenon, but a uniting of the totality of two personalities. In marriage, we are one flesh spiritually by vow, economically by sharing, logistically by adjusting time and agreeing on the disbursement of all life's resources, experientially by trudging through the dark valleys and standing victoriously on the peaks of success, and sexually by the bonding of our bodies.
>
> — Dr. Louis Evans, Jr.

This is a fitting analogy for marriage. A strong one-flesh marriage resists the wedge that the enemy tries to drive in. "And do not give the devil a foothold" (Ephesians 4:27 NLT). Once the devil is able to get a wedge started in a relationship, he keeps pounding away. Unless the couple becomes aware of and consciously removes the wedge, they remain vulnerable to attack. They may be able to survive in a tenuous state for an extended period of time, but at some point a blow will come that will split the couple apart.

Living Day to Day as One Flesh

Let's compare your physical body to a one-flesh marriage. Your body is comprised of many different parts, but they work seamlessly together under the common direction of your brain. You don't have to tell your lungs to take in air, nor do you need to convince your heart to pump blood. These things happen naturally on an ongoing basis without thinking. But your body also knows how to react to various stimuli as well. As an example, if your leg itches, your hand scratches it. The hand doesn't argue that the problem is irrelevant, nor does it think itself above performing such an action. The hand satisfies a need felt by the leg. In a one-flesh marriage you will find there are things you naturally do for one another. And there are times when you have a need that should only be met by your spouse and vice-versa. Satisfying these needs should become as natural as your hand scratching your leg.

If something is out of reach of your hand, your legs will move your body so that it will be closer. In this case, the legs are enabling the hand to accomplish something it couldn't attain on its own. In your marriage you will find times when your spouse has a desire to achieve something but requires your help to do so. This is a beautiful thing. It is not that either of you alone is weak or unable to accomplish things, but together you can do so much more than what either of you could do on your own.

If you are walking on uneven ground, you might stumble and twist your ankle. Without thinking you'll begin to limp, putting additional weight on your good ankle to protect the other while it is injured. Over time as your ankle heals, the limp will subside, and you will begin to walk normally again. There will be times in your marriage when you will be called to carry an additional burden for your spouse until they can take it back on themselves. This could happen during a time of grief, job loss, physical disease, or injury. Whatever the cause, your spouse will not be operating at full efficiency. Just as your body limps, you will be called on to carry the additional burden until your spouse is fully healed.

When functioning as designed, the human body works together seamlessly with all of its disparate parts. Likewise, each part understands that the other parts have a specific function, and they don't try to replicate those functions. The eyes don't try to hear, nor does the tongue try to see. No one part considers itself as more or less important than the other parts. They each respect and trust that the other parts will do their job and that the whole one-flesh body will benefit as a result. A marriage is no different. Each of you has different strengths and gifts. Over time you will learn to seamlessly rely on each other and to support each other as needed.

Sustaining a One Flesh Relationship

God created the world and everything in it. This includes all laws of nature. The second law of thermodynamics speaks of entropy. In laymen's terms, entropy is a concept stating that anything in a state of order will naturally seek a state of disorder. In other words, if left alone, things never get better—they naturally begin to deteriorate. Here's a great example of this. A high-end restaurant near our house went out of business several months ago. This was a classy looking place that customers once found very inviting. It's amazing to me what this same place looks like less than a year later now that is has been abandoned. The parking lot is cracked, huge potholes have emerged, the lawn is overgrown, and the once manicured bushes now look like crazy jungle plants. Shutters on the wall have come off their hinges, and there are visible problems with the roof. This building went from an exclusive restaurant to a decaying structure very quickly once no one cared for it anymore. As entropy denotes, nothing in life gets better or even stays "as is" without ongoing attention and effort.

There are forces that strive to drive one-flesh marriages apart. Sometimes these forces are more obvious than others. Complacency and neglect (entropy) are the single biggest challenges that work to tear couples apart. Never take your marriage for granted. We live in a culture where we are very busy and frankly have more things on our plate than we could ever effectively manage. We find ourselves in a fire-fighting mode where our attention is consumed by the urgent issues, and the merely important things go untouched.

- "I know my wife has had a bad day and needs to talk, but I have to get our son to his baseball game."
- "I know she was planning a special dinner tonight, but I have a project due on Friday. I'm going to have to work late again."
- "I know he wants sex, but I'm so tired from dealing with the kids all day. I couldn't possibly muster the energy."

These are all common marriage scenarios. Couples that live like this are not intentionally abandoning their relationship but are allowing cracks to open that can become severe over time. Couples in strong, healthy marriages put considerable time and effort into meeting the needs of their spouse. They take note when something small is wrong and tend to it before it gets out of hand. One-flesh couples are aware of their partner's moods, health, and feelings. They don't wait to be told there's a problem. They notice early and react. Don't let this overwhelm you. It's not about performing incredible feats of romance or rescue. It's about paying attention and doing appropriate (sometimes small) actions all along the way.

Optimizing Your One Flesh Relationship

A shocking marriage goes beyond creating and maintaining a one-flesh relationship. Couples here are dedicated to helping one another become all that God intends for them to be. Looking beyond their own needs, interests, and priorities, they join the vision that their partner has for their lives. They fully understand that when their spouse is reaching their Godly potential, the marriage is blessed as a result.

I know a couple that has two young boys. In the beginning Dad had a flourishing career as an engineer with a major company in town. Mom was staying at home to help raise the kids. But while she was there, she chose to start a home-based business that took off and began to grow. While he was fully engaged with his own job, he supported her on nights and weekends by watching the kids so she could focus on growing her business. Within a couple of years it had grown to the point that he left his corporate job to join her. They now both work in the new business, sharing the responsibility for both the business and the parenting.

Author Lou and his wife Sara had been married for a few years when she recognized Lou's call and passion for pastoral ministry. She encouraged him to the point of a loving appeal in a meeting with their pastor. Lou was challenged by both Sara and their pastor to attend seminary, which necessitated a family move to a major city and a huge leap of financial faith. While Lou worked and attended classes in Dallas (both full time), Sara managed the home, clearing the path for him to study. Their seminary experience was a one-flesh experience just as their twenty-five years in ministry has been.

We are called to be our spouse's biggest supporter. They need to be able to rely on us in all circumstances and to know we are behind them both physically and emotionally. When they are down, we are to lift them up—even to the point of sacrificing our own needs. When they celebrate, we celebrate with them. Their success is our success. We mutually submit to each other to give our spouse the opportunity to shine as they use their gifts and talents. This is an incredible environment to live in, and every couple should strive to get there. The key is to realize that we sometimes have to subordinate our own desires and goals in order to support our partners.

It's not easy to put the needs of our spouse ahead of our own. Until now your own needs have always come first. Begin praying about this now. Pray that God will help you to recognize your spouse as being one flesh with you. Pray that you will be able to prioritize them and their needs ahead of your own. This is not something you have to do on your own. God wants you to be fulfilled in a blessed marriage. Through his strength and guidance he will help you to look beyond yourself. With time this will become as natural to you as scratching your own knee when it itches.

There are many documented cases of long-term married couples dying within a short time of one another. It's known as the widowhood effect. Nicholas Christakis of Harvard and Felix Elwert of the University of Wisconsin–Madison conducted a study and published a paper in 2008. Their research suggested that within the three months after one spouse dies, the chance that the other will follow is anywhere from thirty to ninety percent. "The death of a spouse, for whatever reason, is a significant threat to health and poses a substantial risk of death by whatever cause," they conclude. It seems that you can in fact die from a broken heart.

Allowing Our Spouses to Complete Us

I once had a boss that told me, "If you and I agree on everything, I have no need for you whatsoever." Having previously worked for some individuals that were looking for the proverbial "yes men," his comment caught me off guard. Was he really expecting me to challenge him on everything? I came to learn in time the answer to that was no. He was not looking for me to be argumentative or to challenge his every thought. But when I had a legitimately unique perspective, he wanted me to share it. It's not that he would abandon his original thinking to adopt mine, but it would typically lead to a spirited discussion that would often result in an outcome superior to either of our original thoughts.

God is not bringing you and your fiancé together to increase your personal capacity. In other words, you are not marrying yourself. You are marrying another person that God has wired with different skills, gifts, and a personal calling. Over time you will learn to utilize these differences for the greater good of the relationship. If you as a couple are asked to do something, you will intuitively know which of you is better equipped to deliver. Capitalizing on your individual strengths will provide your marriage with synergy, exceeding what either of you could accomplish alone.

When Lou performs premarital counseling, he has the couples take a few simple personality tests. In his experience it is a rare thing for a couple's personalities to match. They are more typically complementary. One is often the "kite" and the other the "string." When the two are combined, they both soar.

But that doesn't happen overnight. The reality is that you were initially attracted to your fiancé because there was something different about them that intrigued you. You became a student of them, working hard to understand who they really were and what made them tick. You watched their every move; you analyzed their every sentence. Part of you was looking for reasons to move forward while another part was looking for reasons to get them out of your life. As the relationship developed, you became more and more infatuated with them, and you began to fall in love. It's as if you couldn't spend enough time with them. You eventually decided to get engaged and ultimately married.

During the honeymoon phase of marriage, everything will seem perfect, and you will see no flaws in your spouse. You'll find yourself in the perfect relationship that you can't imagine getting any better. Unfortunately, that feeling won't last forever. In time normalcy will resume, and your attention will shift from your spouse back to yourself. As the honeymoon phase begins to ebb, you will start to notice little things about your spouse that bother you. The differences between you may transform from endearing qualities to irritants. Often times couples spend the rest of their marriage trying to "fix" their spouse by getting them to think and behave more like themselves.

Most people are egocentric enough to believe that they are the definition of "normal." Anyone who thinks or acts differently from them is an aberration. If you are a detailed, planning type of a person, it may frustrate you that your spouse is a dreamer who can always see the big picture but may be oblivious as to how to get there. Likewise, your spouse may be a highly social person that loves to be around people while you prefer to spend time alone or just as a couple. These or other similar situations can be a cause of stress and conflict within a relationship if they are not acknowledged and managed.

It takes a lot of self-confidence and self-awareness to recognize your own strengths and shortcomings. It is much easier to initially connect with an individual that thinks and acts like you do. There is minimal conflict, it is easy to agree on issues, and planning for the future is a breeze. Though this may seem like an ideal relationship, the reality is that God may have brought you a partner that is considerably different from yourself. And that is perfectly okay.

No matter how similar or dissimilar you and your future spouse may be, a Godly marriage should incorporate the gifts and talents of each of you. When you respect your spouse as your equal (and sometimes opposite) partner, you will come to appreciate the fact that God has given them a perspective different from your own. You have to put aside your personal pride, which foolishly tells you that you alone know what is best. Working together to combine the two perspectives will typically lead to a far better result than either of you alone could provide.

Jerry worked with a couple that illustrates this beautifully. Tom and Lois (not their real names) met through a young singles group at church. Lois is a driven person, always striving for the next goal. She has a college degree and is on a path of rapid career growth at her company. Tom is very laid back and relaxed. He too has a college degree but has remained in an entry level job at his company for several years. He appreciates the low-stress nature of his job and is perfectly content to stay there. These two fell in love, both infatuated with the personality that the other had. Lois loved Tom's ability to remain stress-free and found herself relaxed around him. Likewise, Tom appreciated Lois's drive and ambition. The two together seemed to be the perfect and complete package.

In the first five years of marriage they had two children. Their lives seemed complete. But it started to bother Lois that while she had received three promotions during that time, Tom was still in his same job. From her perspective he was not living up to his potential and needed to strive harder to get ahead. Tom came home one day from work and casually mentioned that his boss had offered him a new opportunity that would come with a substantial raise. Tom gave it brief consideration, then turned it down. The new job would require him to manage a team of people, and Tom did not want to take on the burden and responsibility of overseeing other people's lives. When Lois heard this, she went ballistic. She couldn't believe he had turned down such an opportunity. She called him lazy and unmotivated. She began to think she deserved better. At the same time Tom saw her as being overly domineering and critical, thinking that he should not have to put up with such persistent nagging.

The good news is that this couple was able to work things out, and they are now on a better path. But you see how they went exactly through the process described above. They fell in love based on their differences, but in time those very traits nearly tore them apart. Hopefully by now you see where this is going. This couple needs each other. Both will push the other out of their respective comfort zones, but the result should be ultimately satisfying to each. They've had to learn to recognize and utilize each other's gifts to their collective advantage.

Summary

God designed us as humans, and he originated the concept of marriage. As you come together in covenant marriage with him, you become one flesh. There are many blessings associated with becoming one flesh. You learn to love and support your spouse unlike any other person. When you are weak, they can be strong. Together you have gifts and abilities far exceeding what you had on your own. Putting aside the self and embracing your one flesh will allow you to fully appreciate these blessings.

Discussion Questions

1. Notice that in Genesis the woman is called a helper, and in Hebrews the Lord is also called a helper. What insights can you gather from this?

2. In your own words, describe how the grafting of two trees to a rootstock is a visual of a one flesh concept. What insights do you take away?

3. Think about your spouse and your differences in personality, temperament, and more. How do you complete each other?

4. This chapter shared the idea of optimizing your one-flesh relationship. What are your spouse's dreams for the future? How can you support them in pursuing their dream?

CHAPTER 3
BUT WAIT, WHAT IF...?
HONESTLY, I HAVE QUESTIONS

You make a lot of decisions over the course of your lifetime; some are bigger than others. Buying a new car requires more thought and research than buying a new pair of shoes. But even with the magnitude of the car decision, you know it won't last forever—at some point you will be in the market again for a different car. Marriage is different. You are expected to stand before God and everyone and commit to another person that you will be with them until "death do us part." That's a really big decision, but you don't have to make it alone.

Seek out and receive God's direction and blessing, and this will be the most amazing relationship you enter into. The high divorce rate in our country directly reflects couples acting on their own without God's input or guidance. It is important to realize good marriages aren't the result of luck in finding the right partner. They're the result of couples who work daily at walking openly and humbly before God and with each other.

Contemplating marriage can be unnerving. I've never met an engaged person without some doubt or fear in their mind as to their impending commitment, and that's perfectly natural. This is not a decision that should be made lightly, but it should not be avoided due to uncertainty either. Typically concerns boil down to three basic questions.

1. Should we get married?
2. Are we ready for marriage?
3. Is he/she the one?

The following sections will provide information in an effort to help you work through these questions in your mind.

Should We Get Married?

In today's culture the concept of marriage seems outdated to many. Though their parents and grandparents married, young couples question whether it is still a relevant concept. A high percentage of young people today come from broken homes where they experienced the divorce of their parents. They lived through the grief and heartache and are reluctant to put their own kids through that in the future. As a result, cohabitation (living together unmarried) has increased dramatically. Unlike past generations, couples today have to wrestle with the question of whether to get married or simply move in together.

Living together before marriage has become widely accepted both outside and inside the church. The number of couples living together unmarried increased twenty percent in the ten-year period between 2007 and 2016. More than half of these couples are aged thirty-five or younger. Whereas only a few decades ago this practice was widely condemned, a recent Barna study[8] shows that sixty-five percent of American adults (forty-one percent of whom are practicing Christians) believe cohabitation is generally a good idea. A whopping seventy-two percent of millennials are proponents of cohabitation. The bulk

---

[8] Barna June 24, 2016 "Majority of Americans now believe in cohabitation"

of adults studied believe that living together is a "rite of passage" in the path to marriage, stressing the importance of testing a couple's compatibility before a long-term commitment is made. It seems cohabitation has become the new norm.

I've heard young Christian couples argue that the Bible doesn't specifically mention cohabitation, and therefore it must be okay. The reality is that the Bible only refers to sex in two regards: married sex and sexual sin. While it may not be a culturally popular mode of thinking in this day and age, living together in a sexual manner prior to marriage is *sin*. In his letter to the church at Thessalonica, Paul writes: "God's will is for you to be holy, so stay away from all sexual sin" (1 Thessalonians 4:3 NLT).

God wants us to stay away from all sin, but it is interesting he specifically calls out sexual sin in this verse. Paul goes on to warn against living in lustful passion as the pagans do. He is clearly drawing distinction between how we as God's people should live as compared with nonbelievers. In the book of Hebrews Paul goes on to write: "Give honor to marriage and remain faithful to one another in marriage. God will surely judge people who are immoral and those who commit adultery" (Hebrews 13:4 NLT). Other translations say to "keep the marriage bed pure," further emphasizing the importance of sexual purity in marriage.

This verse clearly says to "give honor to marriage," not to "give honor to love…" Love is a key part of marriage, but without a covenant commitment love alone does not justify entering into a sexual relationship. The Bible defines this as sin. It would seem the once distinguishing line between believers and nonbelievers has all but disappeared in this regard. We wrote earlier about the importance of covenant in marriage, explaining that any couple entering into a marriage covenant with God will receive His blessings. But couples living in an active state of unconfessed sin should not expect God to honor or enter into any such arrangement.

Aside from Christian values, is cohabitation really a good idea? Dozens of studies have been done on couples living together outside of marriage. Their results vary considerably, but there are a few points that nearly all of them agree on.

- Only about fifty percent of cohabitating couples end up getting married.
- The divorce rate for couples that cohabitated before marriage is higher than those who didn't.
- Both men and women that commit to cohabitation are more likely to cheat on each other than married couples.

There appears to be no evidence that "test-driving" a relationship prior to marriage improves the odds of marital success.

Statistically speaking, if you are engaged and reading this book, there is a good chance you are currently living with your fiancé. You tell yourself you're in love, and you're going to get married anyway, so why does it matter?

Let's take a look at how Jesus dealt with this topic in the book of John. In this story we find Jesus walking to Galilee. Along the way he stops to rest at a well in Samaria where he meets a Samaritan woman. He asks her for a drink, and a conversation ensues. He tells the woman of his identity and then instructs her as follows:

> "Go and get your husband," Jesus told her. "I don't have a husband," the woman replied. Jesus said, "You're right! You don't have a husband—for you have had five husbands, and you aren't even married to the man you're living with now. You certainly spoke the truth!"
>
> —John 4:16-18 NLT

There are many takeaways from this passage. Though in earlier verses we see Jesus offering life, truth, and grace to this woman, here he is pointing out that she is living in an unmarried state and has been doing so for quite some time. As we've explained before, a marriage is not merely a legal contract. It is a covenant relationship. In a Christian marriage ceremony promises are first made with God, then with each other. When the Bible states "The two shall become one…" it is implying a commitment to a God-focused journey. Without this commitment cohabitation is simply a self-centered means of manipulation, convenience, and comfort to varying degrees.

I don't know of any couples that decided to cohabitate before becoming sexually active. Often times sex occurs early on in the relationship. Whereas the emphasis used to be on waiting until marriage to have sex, many now believe it is important only to wait until the third date to do so. Once the couple decides they are "sexually compatible," moving in together becomes the first real stage of commitment to one another. There may be a sense of practicality about it. For example, she gets tired of waking up at his place without a toothbrush or a change of clothes. But there is an awareness that moving in together is a huge step in the relationship. Couples will realize it becomes much harder to separate once they've begun to acquire shared possessions or pets.

Beyond pure convenience, men and women initiate moving in together for very different reasons. From a woman's perspective, if she can get the man to live with her, she believes it will push him toward marriage. It's as if they are on a journey and moving in together is a big step toward that destination. Oddly, this very act can delay a man's desire for marriage. Once a couple is sexually active in the same home, the motivation to marry for most men drops. There is minimal perceived benefit beyond where the relationship is now.

Most men approach this from a different perspective. When they initiate or agree to move in together, they do not want to lose what they currently enjoy. They want the readily available sexual pleasure that results, but they are not ready to commit to their partner, to decide they are ultimately "the one." If men were certain of this, they would propose marriage. Instead they choose to keep their options open. While men would never say this openly, it is in the back of their minds. It's as if they're thinking, "You're good for now, but I reserve the right to move on should someone better come along." How can you truly have a thriving relationship if one of the partners is always considering other options?

I know several couples that have lived together for a considerable time. At some point they announce they are engaged. Social media lights up with congratulations and excitement. But ask these same couples when the wedding date is, and they'll admit they haven't decided that yet. Some of these couples stay engaged for years without ever going through the ceremony. I get the sense in most of these cases that the woman increased the pressure on the man to get married, and he acquiesced to keep her happy. You see the aforementioned motives clearly come in to play in these situations.

I believe if more couples understood these underlying motivations and looked beyond the immediate picture toward a longer-term perspective, cohabitation rates would decrease. One couple told me, "We're already living together, and we're going to get married. We're both believers, so we're already married in God's eyes." I don't believe for a second that they were already married in God's eyes. In the example of this couple, a covenant with God was never discussed or implied. They were living in an unconfessed state of sin.

You may be asking, "If I'm living with my fiancé now, does that mean our marriage is doomed from the start?" Nowhere in the Bible does God prioritize sins. Cohabitation is no worse than any other sin, and through grace any sin can absolutely be forgiven. However, it is important to note that while openly living in a state of sin a couple may find their prayers are hindered.

"If I had cherished sin in my heart, the Lord would not have listened" (Psalms 66:18 NLT).

We've already established that sex outside of marriage is sin. It only makes sense that you cannot enter into a covenant with God if communication has been disrupted due to unconfessed or ongoing sin.

Let's make this point very clearly. If you are currently living with or having sex with your partner outside of marriage, *stop doing so*. Move out! Move back in with your parents, move in with a friend of the same sex, or even rent your own apartment.

Seek God's forgiveness for your sin. Then look forward to the day when you can reengage with your partner in a new covenant relationship. Your sexual sin can and will be forgiven. But God will not enter into a covenant relationship with you while you continue to engage in sinful practices.

I've had people tell me this thinking is unrealistic in this day and age. At what point has God changed His mind about what is and is not acceptable in His eyes? God is the same today as He was a hundred or even a thousand years ago. If you want to receive His blessings, you need to honor His standards and not try to justify your own.

I mentioned earlier that the average time to plan a wedding in the US is around fourteen months. It is likely this duration directly correlates to couples cohabitating. There's no sense of urgency to hold a wedding when you're already living as if you are married. When you are already living together, your wedding is primarily a large, showy party. If your preferred venue or band is unavailable on your desired date, you're willing to wait six months until they are. What's the difference? On the other hand, if you are waiting until marriage to begin or to resume having sex, you will have a much higher motivation and sense of urgency to get on with the wedding. Preferred venue not available? You may suddenly be willing to compromise on this point if it means getting to be intimate with your spouse sooner. In my own life I was very excited about getting married and wanted a short engagement as I could barely wait for sex. Had I been living with Tara at the time, I would not have been in any hurry whatsoever.

Are We Ready for Marriage?

One of the most common concerns many couples have when beginning to contemplate marriage is the fundamental question: "How do we know if we're ready?" It is important to realize that the answer to this question depends partly on your current situation. If you are currently living with your partner, you may never feel ready as only fifty percent of cohabitating couples actually wed. You will not feel God's direction if you are in this state, so you'll be making the decision solely on your own.

Assuming you are not living together or have stopped living together, faith becomes an important element that should drive your decision. You may never feel completely ready or find that the timing is perfect. Pray both together and individually in an effort to seek God's perfect will. Asking for God's will is very different from asking Him to bless a plan that you've already decided on. It is important that you are willing to listen for His answer. God may be nudging you to move forward, but your own hesitations and fears are holding you back. On the flip side, He may be placing cautions in your mind that should not be ignored. The following questions are a good place to start both within your own mind as well as in prayer.

- Do I feel that God has brought this person into my life?
- Do we have God's blessing on this union?
- Do I love my partner with all my heart?
- Can I commit to being with them until we're separated by death?

It is important to deal with each of these questions seriously and independently. There may be ulterior motives for wanting to wed that can blind a person to the truth. Be careful if you find yourself in any of the following situations.

- I am lonely, and being with someone is better than being alone.
- I need to escape my current reality—getting married will allow me to do that.
- I've only known them for a short period of time, but it was love at first sight.
- If I don't marry them, I'll lose them to someone else.
- They are very wealthy or well-connected or powerful. I will benefit from being their spouse.
- I'm getting older, so I better take what I can get.

There are surely other situations that are equally troubling, but these should provide you with some guidance. In each of these instances, there is a very selfish motive for getting married. Couples who marry with these justifications typically don't do well over the long run. Once married they find that their fundamental issues have not been resolved, and their spouse is not providing the cure-all that was expected.

How Do I Know He or She Is the One?

When deciding if your partner is the one you want to spend the rest of your life with, you need to consider compatibility. This is not about living together or sexual compatibility but rather understanding who your partner is, what drives them forward, and the values they hold. I've heard it said that women marry men with the hope of changing them, and men marry women, hoping they will never change. Both are disappointed. There is much truth in this humorous statement. Understanding and accepting your partner for who they are is a huge step in compatibility.

Studies show that if couples date for at least one year before marrying, they have a lower risk of divorce than couples that marry quickly. The primary reason for this is that issues naturally arise as couples spend time together. Diversity of activities spent during this time has a big influence on this. As an example, a couple could spend two years dating, but if every date consisted of going to the same type of restaurant and a movie, they would learn less about each other than a couple sharing a wider range of experiences over a shorter amount of time. Diversity of timing is also important. If your dating has been limited to Friday and Saturday nights, you may be surprised what your partner is like on a Saturday morning. I knew a couple that dated for a year before they were married. They seemed compatible in almost every way. But due to their work schedules they primarily dated on weekend nights and the occasional Sunday afternoon. She knew he loved to golf and did so most Saturday mornings with a group of his friends, but that never impacted her, so she gave it little attention. She was excited about starting their lives together and looked forward to taking day trips and weekend adventures. Once married she was unpleasantly surprised when she found that he had no intentions of altering his Saturday morning schedule to do something other than golf.

It's not that you have to be completely aligned in terms of your likes and dislikes, but it is important to understand where you are similar and where you are different. If one of you dreams of a life of high adventure and the other prefers to stay home with a good book, you are probably headed toward long-term discontent.

I (Jerry) will give you a personal example. I have always been an adventurous eater. I love to try foods from all over the world and will seldom turn down the opportunity to try something new. This was an important criterion for me as I considered compatibility with a potential partner all the way back to high school. I recall one particular date I had with a girl I was infatuated with. She was beautiful and funny, and I was strongly drawn to her. I finally mustered the nerve to ask her out. When she agreed to go, I was ecstatic! We had eaten at fast food restaurants several times as part of a school group we were both involved in. My hope was to impress her, so I took her to a nicer restaurant. Keep in mind that I was only in high school, so "nicer" simply implied having a menu instead of ordering from the counter.

We were seated and given our menus. I immediately started calling out items I thought sounded delicious and was excited to try. Her reply stopped me dead in my tracks. "That sounds gross. How could anyone ever eat that?" This led to a conversation where she admitted the only thing on this six-page menu she would eat was chicken nuggets. I knew at that moment this would be our one and only date.

Before you write me off as a food snob, let me contrast this situation with dating (my now wife) Tara. Tara was raised in a home where meat and potatoes were the standard. She had not been exposed to many different types of foods and was very happy in her comfort zone. When I took her to a similar restaurant, she expressed a willingness to try things she'd not had before. She didn't like everything, but she was open to tasting them. Fast forward a few decades, and today she loves unique foods almost as much as I do. The compatibility here was not in the fact she loved the same foods as I did but rather that she had an attitude of "willingness to try" unfamiliar things. I knew I couldn't spend the rest of my life eating chicken nuggets, but with Tara I sensed this would never be a problem. And it hasn't been. Imagine the conflict and frustration that would have surfaced had I never taken the first girl out to dinner or had we simply grabbed fast food after doing something else we both enjoyed. While people do change over time, don't assume you can change them. I ran into the girl I mentioned before at a class reunion a few years ago. She is still the picky eater she was in her youth. She is now married to a nice guy who shares her general dislike for food. They seem perfect together!

Most engaged couples feel like they have learned everything they need to know about their partners. This is especially true if they have been dating for an extended period of time, but even couples that have become engaged after a short-term relationship often assume they know everything they need to. However, in most cases couples know a great deal about a fairly narrow segment of their partner's life. This is perfectly natural. Dating is a time of both selling and buying. You want to make the best impression you can in order to sell yourself, and at the same time you are evaluating your partner as a potential spouse.

You have probably encountered a sleazy salesperson at some point, someone that was trying to downplay the flaws or shortcomings of a product in hopes of making a sale. I'm not suggesting your partner has done this, but there are certain areas or topics that are often avoided in the dating phase. It could be these issues surfaced briefly in the past but were dropped quickly to avoid awkwardness. Nobody wants to provide a laundry list of issues for fear they will scare their partner off. But prior to marriage it is important to surface any issues that could cause stress or conflict later. Once you see your partner "warts and all" and still want to marry them, you should be good to go. Exploring these topics may surface concerns or even cause a couple to rethink their engagement. If that happens, *consider it a blessing*. If you have areas of incompatibility, it is much better to surface them now than once you've wed. It's not an easy path to take, but it is sure preferable to the alternative.

The following questions will help you identify areas where you might encounter conflict or difficulties in your marriage. While that may sound inherently negative, knowing where a challenge lies in advance makes it much easier to deal with than stumbling onto that same challenge unexpectedly. Answer these questions independently and then share with your partner. Doing this will ensure that you get to real answers and feelings rather than jumping on the "me too" bandwagon.

The first question encourages you to share your priorities with one another.

List your top five priorities in life (moving forward) from most important to least important.

Answers typically include some of the following: career, family, faith, wealth, security, fame, influence, etc. Be completely honest with yourself when answering. What really motivates you? What keeps you going? What would you feel that you had sacrificed if you didn't achieve it?

When you share with your partner, understand it is not critical to be fully aligned in your answers. It is important to understand and support each other's priorities. Once you have shared answers, talk about your similarities and differences. How can they work together? Where might differences raise issues? As an example, if one of you lists career as a top priority but the other lists family, what could this look like? If one of you places faith at the top and the other doesn't list it at all, what will that look like? Don't enter into marriage with the assumption that your partner values everything the exact same way you do. Use this information to help plan your future together. If you see a major conflict (e.g. you value family and children as a top priority, but your partner feels that kids would hinder their career), it is critical you work through this prior to getting married. Do not assume you can simply work this out later or that your partner will come around.

The next question deals with your respective visions for your marriage.

What do you see your marriage looking like in ten, thirty, and fifty years?

Unlike the first question, this is a topic that you should be able to seek alignment on. While the odds of accuracy in your answers are low (meaning that ten, thirty, and fifty years into the marriage will not look like what you anticipate now), it is important you create a shared vision. It is much easier to make important short-term decisions if you both share a vision of where you are headed as a couple.

Breaking the vision into these time segments will also help you map out the overall direction of your marriage. For example, you might both agree you'll pursue individual careers for the first five or so years of marriage but then switch to a one-career family once you have children. Knowing this will cause you to treat spending and investment differently than if you assume you'll both work forever and then change your mind later.

The third question is intended to prevent any unpleasant surprises that might otherwise arise in your marriage.

What baggage do you bring into the marriage?

We all have baggage, and like it or not, we bring it into our marriages. This can take on various forms and will be different for every person. The important thing is to acknowledge this, communicate it, and plan to deal with it effectively. You don't want to be surprised when something significant arises unexpectedly.

Lou tells the story of a lady he knew from church. She was a strong Christian woman that fell in love with a man and was married soon thereafter. They had their dream wedding and then left for a honeymoon cruise. Upon returning to the US, her new husband was met at the port of entry by federal agents that immediately put him into handcuffs. Unbeknownst to her he had embezzled hundreds of thousands of dollars from a past employer. Clearly he had baggage of which she was unaware.

What are the things from your past that could surface or continue to drive your beliefs and behaviors to this day? The following are examples of questions that may or may not pertain to you, but use them to stimulate thinking in regard to your own past.

- I was a victim of physical, sexual, or verbal abuse.
- I struggle with addictions (chemical, alcohol, shopping, pornography, etc.).
- I have a criminal record.
- I have a child from a past relationship.
- I have an extreme fear of _____.
- I am unwilling to do or try certain things.
- I am unwilling to go to certain places.
- I have experienced trauma in the past.
- I have strong political beliefs.

You get the idea. This is not intended to be an exhaustive list, but it should serve as a conversation starter. Many of these issues have probably surfaced and been discussed over the course of a healthy dating relationship. It is important to understand that answering "yes" to any of these does not mean your relationship is doomed. Rather, it is simply important to understand these issues before you are confronted with them unexpectedly. As an example, admitting you got a long-lost girlfriend pregnant years ago is a tough conversation to have. But having that conversation now will be much easier than having that grown child ring your doorbell in the future, proclaiming you are their father.

Jeremy and Claire were engaged to be married after dating for two years. The weekend of their wedding arrived, and they had numerous family and friends that had come into town for the big event. The night before the ceremony Claire went to Jeremy's house (which she would be moving into) to drop some items off. He was out running errands, so he was not at home. She saw his computer was on and went over to check on an email she was expecting. When she "woke up" the computer, she was astonished to see a pornographic image on the screen. While investigating she went into his browser history and saw he had spent considerable time on multiple porn sites as far back as she could see. This was a side of Jeremy she did not know existed. She decided she couldn't marry a man with such an addiction and called the wedding off. Jeremy had no choice but to call all of his friends and family and explain there would be no wedding the next day.

Sexual History

You don't have to bring up every person you've kissed since junior high school, but if there is something or someone from your past that could affect your relationship in the future, it should be shared. Past, unconfessed lovers have a way of awkwardly reappearing at inopportune moments. More than half of couples bring a sexual history into their marriages. This is another indication of how our culture has departed from God's original design. While this will be an uncomfortable topic, it is important to share your sexual past with your future spouse. Couples often ask, "How much do I share?" The answer is: "As much as your partner wants to know." It is important that your spouse can trust you have not held anything back and know you are not carrying any secrets. Once they are sure everything they care about is known, they can deal with the information and begin to reconcile it in their own minds. If one of you has a sexual past but the other has saved yourself for marriage, this can be an especially tough issue to wrestle through.

God designed us to be exclusive with our spouse. We want to know the things we've seen and done together have not been shared with anyone else. We shudder at the thought of comparisons. We wonder if we're good enough, big enough, or sexy enough. Our insecurity will lead us to wonder if they really prefer their past lover to us. It is critical to understand that while sex is an important aspect of marriage, it is not the only aspect. Once you have confessed your past to your partner it is important to put that history *behind* you. As you enter into a covenant relationship with God and your spouse, you begin anew. Jesus showed grace in forgiving your sins—you owe that same grace to your spouse. Once forgiven you don't bring up past relationships, and you don't make comparisons (either verbally or mentally).

I (Jerry) worked with a young couple on premarital counseling. For the purpose of this story, I'll call them Jim and Sue (not their real names). They are both devout believers firmly committed to the Lord. But as we went through the process, I came to learn they both had a sexual history. Interestingly, they committed to remain chaste until marriage, but neither were virgins. They were open with each other about their pasts and were willing and able to forgive one another. They were very excited about becoming sexually active once married, and the passion they were building up was quite obvious.

They met in a small city in the Midwest where they would live after the wedding. This is Jim's hometown, but Sue moved in from another state. One week during counseling I could see there was considerable tension between the two of them. As I probed for the reason, I came to learn that while they were at dinner the night before, a young lady came up to their table to talk to them. She clearly knew Jim and was extremely friendly. She was excited to meet Sue and began wishing them all the best in their future relationship. It was only after dinner when Sue learned this particular woman was a part of Jim's sexual history. While in her mind she had forgiven Jim, she suddenly feared that this other woman would be an ongoing presence in the small city where they would live.

It's interesting. Jim did nothing wrong in this situation, but Sue was quite upset. Over the course of our session together, I was able to remind her that she too had a past, and it was not fair to be angry with Jim simply because of their proximity to this woman. The same situation would be true if the two of them were to move to her hometown or if her past lover suddenly decided to move here. At this point Sue had to make a choice. Could she truly forgive Jim and trust he no longer had feelings toward this other woman? She came to understand her choice could not be conditional but needed to be absolute. Jim assured her there were no residual feelings toward this other woman and that his love was strictly focused on Sue. It turned out to be a very healing session, one I am glad happened before the wedding took place.

Perhaps you have no sexual history prior to your current partner, but you have been sexually active with them. You may question the long-term viability of your relationship, but guilt is driving you to move toward marriage. If this is the case, I strongly recommend that you mutually agree to put a hold on your sexual activities for now and evaluate your relationship from an objective, nonphysical perspective. If guilt is primarily moving you forward, it would be better to end things now than to enter into a false covenant and end up divorcing later. If on the other hand you find you still long to be together (even while abstaining), then you can get right with God, enter into a lasting covenant, and enjoy a long and fruitful marriage together.

Dating should be a time of exploration and discovery. You want to uncover as many preferential differences as you can. As issues arise, you have to ask yourself, "Is this something I can live with for the rest of my life?" In many cases you can. Your partner may be a night owl, and you are an early bird. While this may cause stress from time to time, it's also something you can learn to use to your advantage. But in your life you may have some non-negotiables. These are areas where you feel like you would have to totally compromise your desires or wishes in order to stay together. These are red flags if they exist in your relationship. Before you go any further together, get these out on the table and discuss them. Look past today and envision a future together. How will these things play out? As an example, imagine you are a physically active, athletic person who loves to explore the outdoors through hiking and backpacking, but your partner is more sedentary and prefers staying indoors with a good book. In fact, they don't like to be out in nature at all. Ask yourself, "What do future vacations look like? How about a getaway weekend?" If the only solution you can envision is to each do your own thing and take individual trips, that is not a good situation. You will find yourself in a life of negotiation and compromise. If, however, your partner expresses a willingness to try your activities, and you in turn are willing to have some fewer active times, then you may both benefit.

When you think about your relationship, you can think in terms of three categories.

1. What you *know* that you *know*
2. What you *know* that you *don't know*
3. What you *don't know* that you *don't know*

The first category is the easiest. This contains all the information you have come to learn about your future spouse. This would include all the things you've been told (e.g. family history, past relationships, career background, expressed likes and dislikes) plus any items you have come to learn through experience or observation (e.g. he's very close to his mother, she has a fear of meeting new people, he has a quick temper). These represent "truths" you can either learn to deal with or avoid. The point is that none of these should surprise you.

The second category is important to explore. This list will include things that are important as well as things that really don't matter. As an example, it is very important to know if your future spouse wants to have children and if so how many. If you know you don't know this, it is critical you find out prior to marriage. If your heart is set on having a large family but they don't want kids, now is the time to find out so you can make decisions accordingly. On the other hand, you may not know if they have ever tried snails. Might be interesting information, but it is not critical to planning a future together.

The third category is the one that can trip you up. It's the things you don't realize you don't know that can come as a terrible surprise. By definition this is not a list you can complete. The goal is to minimize this by learning as much as you can prior to marriage. Per the earlier discussion the one exception to this category is sex. God's intent is for you to discover this together as a married couple. Ideally you are each other's first sexual partners, so you have no preconceived notions about preferences, likes, or dislikes. You are making no mental comparisons with previous partners.

Take off the Blinders

Sometimes we can get caught up in our emotions and blind ourselves to reality. This is especially true when a couple is sexually active, but it is not limited to that. It is important to gain input from God, family, and close friends in terms of how they see your relationship. Many Christian couples that divorce within the first five years of marriage reflect back and realize in hindsight that God may have been trying to get through to them, but they were unwilling to listen.

Both of the authors (Jerry and Lou) have dealt with couples in this situation. Issues existed that could be seen by friends and family ahead of time, but the couples were unable or unwilling to acknowledge them. In each of these situations at least one member of the couple was advised to call things off. They were clearly warned of what lie ahead of them, but they wouldn't hear it. They proceeded to move ahead, assuring everyone things would be fine. "It will work out," they assured their friends. Sure enough these marriages were short lived.

It is important to understand all advice is not equal. I (Jerry) was told by many we were too young to get married—it would never last. Several friends advised we simply move in together and not make such a lasting commitment prematurely. I thank

God nearly forty years later I did not follow that advice as I don't think we would have the same marital blessings we have enjoyed. In hindsight that advice was strictly based on other people's opinions. That is a very different situation than the marriages described earlier. In those cases people close to the couple were bringing up tangible issues such as ongoing deceit, mental instability, or a hidden past that should have been (at a minimum) dealt with prior to marriage.

Summary

Getting married is a big decision. It is natural to have questions or even doubts before it occurs. Take the time leading up to your wedding to discuss your future life together in detail. Unveil any hidden secrets, share your dreams, and talk about topics that you might not have previously addressed. Work through any issues that arise and make sure you have a path moving forward that you can both live with.

Discussion Questions

1. What have been your thoughts on cohabitation to this point? Has Jesus's approach to marriage in John 4:16-17 affected your thoughts on this topic?

2. Why does unconfessed or unrepented sin make a covenant marriage impossible? (See Psalm 66:18.)

3. Have you thoughtfully and prayerfully answered the questions under the heading "Are We Ready for Marriage?"

4. Have you honestly answered the questions under the heading "How Do I Know He or She is the One?"

5. Do you feel comfortable that you are entering into marriage with no hidden secrets or baggage?

PART 2
THINGS TO LEARN BEFORE THE WEDDING

CHAPTER 4
MANAGING EXPECTATIONS -
YOU LIKE TO WHAT?

Assumptions can be dangerous, especially in the area of contemplating marriage. Often times people sense something they are not comfortable with in their partner, but they assume things will work out over time. The time for huge discovery and unpleasant surprises is not after you say, "I do." Tales abound of couples discovering their new spouse has an unexpected child from a past relationship, a surprising mountain of debt, or an unwillingness to participate in activities they assumed would be a part of their future together.

Use the time leading up to marriage to discuss your expectations both as individuals and as a couple. It is far better to discuss and debate your opinions and expectations openly before you are faced with making a decision under a time crunch or forced into a compromise. We all have quirks, histories, opinions, and strange family members. These may not be dealbreakers in terms of the relationship but rather a matter of proactively managing each other's expectations.

In this chapter we will list a variety of topics you should discuss and come to agreement on prior to marriage. This is not intended to be a comprehensive list but rather some basic topics to start discussions. You may find some of these sections don't apply to you and that other unmentioned areas are important. Spend time as a couple working through these topics now; it will prevent considerable stress later on.

Cast a Vision for your Marriage

The best way to manage the expectations of you and your spouse is to discuss and form them together. There's a reason successful companies spend time establishing and communicating a vision. They realize it is virtually impossible to get to a place never imagined in the first place. A vision provides direction moving forward and allows for correction when things veer off course.

Before you can cast a vision for your marriage, you should spend some time creating a vision for yourself. What is it you want to be? What do you want to ultimately leave behind? What do you want to be known for? What values do you hold sacred? It is important you know who you are, what you value, and where you are headed. Take the time to share this with your partner.

As you prepare for marriage, expand your perspective. It's no longer only about you the individual. You are now half of a married couple. Take time to integrate the personal visions each of you have into a new, collective vision created for your marriage. Why is this so critical? Let's look at an example.

Joe is a driven career man. He has risen faster in his company than his peers and has a personal vision of becoming a CEO of a Fortune 100 company. He is a Christ-follower and prides himself on his ethical behavior and his unwillingness to compromise his values to get ahead. His wife Sue is equally driven and runs her own business established several years ago. It has grown considerably, and she now oversees a workforce of over one hundred employees. The two have been married for ten years and have two elementary aged children. Each would say their marriage is "fine," but they don't spend a lot of time together. They have a full-time nanny helping to take care of the kids and the home while they are at work.

While they each have a clear vision of what they are personally seeking in life, they've never taken the time to create a vision for their marriage. While their first few years together seemed blissful, the onset of kids has dominated the little free time they have. Today they live primarily independent lives, coexisting in the same home but mostly seeing each other in passing.

One day Joe comes home with exciting news. He has been offered his first CEO job. It's at a smaller company, but in his mind it's the perfect next step toward his ultimate career goal. The only downside to the offer is that it will require a relocation to the East Coast. Sue's company is based in the Southwest. A move like this would require her to sell the company or hand it off to someone else to run day to day. What happens now?

Let's look at an analogy. Picture two sets of very close train tracks running parallel as far as the eye can see. There's a flatbed rail car on each track. A person stands with one foot on each car. As long as the tracks run perfectly parallel, there is no problem. But over time the tracks begin to diverge slightly, so gradually that it's hard to see they're separating. The person straddling the two cars begins to feel a bit of discomfort as their legs spread apart, but they rationalize this in their mind, convincing themselves it is something they can live with. In time the discomfort becomes all out pain as they are spread too wide. Eventually the person falls off as it is impossible to remain on both cars when they are heading in separate directions.

This is the situation Joe and Sue are in. They both straddle two visions that will inevitably veer apart at some point. When this happens, they have to decide what to do: stay on their own vision (separating them) or completely jump on to the other's vision (causing lasting resentment). Making things worse, they are faced with a decision under the pressure of a deadline. It seems impossible to come up with a solution with which they can both be satisfied.

Having a vision for their marriage could have spared them much of this difficulty. Agreeing that a happy, healthy marriage is first and foremost in each of their minds would have landed them in a different place. With this in mind they might have decided Sue's business was the most "family-friendly" in that it entailed minimal travel whilst growing at a rapid rate. Joe would still be encouraged to be successful in his career with the understanding that there might come a point where he would turn down a promotion requiring relocation in order to support the vision of the marriage and the family. With a vision like this in place, Joe would never have accepted the interview, knowing it would conflict with where they were heading as a couple.

Creating a marital vision is simple, but it's not easy. It takes some heartfelt communication and a willingness to potentially compromise your own dreams in support of your collective ones. Engagement is a great time to go through this exercise. Use the following questions as a starting point for this process.

- What does "success" in marriage look like to the both of you?
- What do you want your marriage to be like in ten, twenty-five, and fifty years?
- What values do you share as a couple that you are unwilling to compromise?
- How can your personal visions fit within the vision for your marriage?
- What type of vision can you envision for your kids someday?

Your vision will be unique to your marriage, so spend some time fleshing this out. Once you have established your vision, it is important to refer back to it on a regular basis. You may find that you want to revise it over time, and that is fine as long as you both are fully on board with the changes. Revisiting it periodically will help you to see if your marriage is on course or if your tracks are starting to diverge slightly. Back to the analogy, it is much easier to make adjustments or corrections before you are in pain or under time pressures.

Honoring God

Assuming you are both Christ-followers, this one should be easy. But again, it is better to discuss than to assume. Once you are married, you will have entered into a covenant relationship that involves both your spouse and God Himself. What practical implications will this have in your relationship?

Twila and Jeremy were engaged. As they went through the premarital counseling process, Jeremy was evasive about a commitment to a Christ centered marriage, but Twila assumed they were on the same page. After the vows were spoken, Jeremy soon became ambivalent about church and then stopped attending altogether. Before long he began to mock his wife's faith commitment. Bad assumptions led to an erosion of the marriage.

Discuss the following as a couple:

Overarching Questions

- Have you each made a personal commitment to accept Christ as your lord and savior?
- Share your testimony of how you came to Christ.
- What long-term, tangible evidence do you see in the life of your fiancé to indicate that a faith walk is important?

Relationship

- What does a God-honoring relationship look like to each of you?
- Do you both agree it is God joining you together as a couple?
- Are you both committed to this relationship for the long run ('til death do you part)?
- Can you agree divorce will never be an option, nor will it be used as a threat?

Church

- What are your views on church?
- Will you attend church on a regular basis? What does regular mean to you?
- What type of church would you look for (denominational, nondenominational, contemporary, traditional, mega-church, small, intimate church, etc.)?
- Will you want to get involved as a volunteer at your church? As individuals or as a couple?
- What is your philosophy on giving?
- How will you raise your children?

Spiritual Growth

- Do you want to pray together?
- Do you want to read and study the Bible together?
- What other dreams do each of you have in this area (going on a mission trip, starting a ministry, serving at a soup kitchen or homeless shelter, etc.)?

Hopefully none of these questions have caused you too much consternation. Discussing and agreeing on these in advance will make the spiritual aspect of your marriage run more smoothly.

It is important to note that agreeing on this list and observing a genuine spiritual walk in your partner does not guarantee you'll never have differences of opinion on other faith topics. You might love one particular church you visit, but your spouse doesn't care for it at all. Or she wants to do daily devotions together in the morning, and he wants to participate in a men's Bible study on Saturday mornings. It is important to listen to one another and come to understand the motivation for each other's preferences or feelings. There will be times when you get your way, and there will be times when you need to willingly compromise. The important thing is to focus on what is best for your marriage from a big picture perspective. Are you agreeing on the essentials? If so, you can learn to give and take on some of the lesser issues.

Shared Dreams and Expectations

As you look towards marriage, you will inevitably find there are a variety of things you both look forward to doing or moving toward. Spending time identifying these will go a long way toward helping you prioritize your lives together and putting plans in place to move forward. You can't outachieve your dreams; if you never dream big, you'll never do big things. This is a great time to fantasize about your life as a married couple. As an example, if you would love to travel to Europe as a couple before you have kids, getting this on your collective radar now will go a long way toward enabling it to happen. Waiting until you're pregnant to share this dream will really constrain your options in terms of schedule and budget.

Examples of collective dreaming questions might include:

- What places do you want to visit someday?
- What does your dream home look like?
- What hobbies might you take up together?
- What challenges and adventures would you like to take on?
- What are some experiences you'd like to try together?
- What type of volunteerism could you do together?
- Is there an older married couple you admire that you want to be like someday?
- Do you have any dreams of furthering your education?

These are merely examples. Feel free to use these but add more of your own as well. The point of this exercise is to get you talking about your collective dreams for the future. Life happens, and circumstances change. The odds that you will complete everything on your list are slim, but write down your answers and store them away. Imagine coming across this list when you celebrate your twenty-fifth wedding anniversary. It will surely put a smile on your faces as you think back to what you aspired to compared to what you've actually accomplished.

Family Expectations

This exercise may sound similar to the previous one, but in reality it is quite different. Whereas the collective dreaming effort encouraged you to imagine a desired future, this exercise focuses on the expectations that each of you currently has for the future in terms of family. Answer the following questions individually and then share your answers with one another. Where you are aligned, move on. But if you see marked differences, initiate a conversation. Your situation and attitudes will change over time, but with good communication you should find they evolve together. The goal of this exercise is to avoid unexpected surprises in regard to your partner's long-held beliefs.

Children

It is important to be aligned not only on whether to have a family but also the numbers of kids, timing, willingness to adopt, etc.

- Do I want to have children? How many children would I like to have?
- Would I be interested in adopting children?
- If yes, I would be willing to adopt a child of another race or from another country?
- If yes, I would be willing to adopt a child with special needs?
- Would I consider being a foster parent?
- I don't want to have our first child before I'm _____ years old.
- I don't want to have my last child after I am _____ years old.
- One of us should be a stay-at-home parent while the children are young.

- If yes, which parent?
- If yes, at what point should the parent return to work?

You may not agree initially on all of these points. Take some time to discuss your differences to see which ones are deeply held and which are strictly opinions held at this time. Differences need not be cause for concern unless the two of you are polar opposites. If you dream of a large family but your partner doesn't want children at all, then you've surfaced a significant issue that could cause tremendous stress in the future. If this is the case, thank God that you discovered this now and not five years into your marriage.

Ron and Betty dreamed of starting a large family soon after they wed. Unfortunately, after attempting to get pregnant for several months, they learned they struggled with infertility. While this was an emotional setback for both of them, they began to pray that God would intervene and solve their issue. While Betty remained unable to become pregnant, they opted to become foster parents with the intention of adopting. Within a couple of years they found themselves with four wonderful sons. While this was not the path they originally intended, they listened for God and found themselves with a large family after all.

Parenting Style

It is important to discuss not only having children but also how you want to raise them. It is critical in marriage that you present a united front to your kids. Otherwise it will be in their nature to try to divide you or to play you against each other. Talk about how you were raised, what you would like to repeat from your upbringing, and what you would like to change. One area to focus on initially is discipline.

- What are your views on discipline techniques?
- Do you believe in spanking?

- What other form(s) of discipline should we use?
- Should all our children be disciplined in the same manner?

Joe did not get married until he was nearly forty. He met Sally, a lovely lady his same age, and they dated for about a year before deciding to wed. Because of their age they decided to start a family right away. Joe was raised in the Midwest in a solid Christian family. His father was a gruff and intimidating man who believed in spanking. He was never abusive, but he was not one to withhold physical punishment when he determined it was merited. Sally was raised in a progressive family in California. They were appalled by the concept of spanking and relied simply on a series of discussions and time-outs in order to modify behavior.

During their engagement Joe and Sally talked about the desire to have children and acknowledged they would need to start a family quickly. They never talked about their backgrounds in terms of how they'd been raised or disciplined as children and how this affected their philosophies toward raising their own children.

Within the first year of their marriage they had a child, and their second followed within fourteen months. They both felt blessed and loved being parents. Their oldest child turned two, an age when parents begin to discipline a child. The first time Joe saw his daughter do something dangerous, he gave her a little swat on the behind and sternly told her "No!" Sally was mortified as she watched him do this. She quickly swept up the crying child, comforted her, and held her away from Daddy. Neither spouse knew what to say to the other.

In time they worked this out and agreed on an approach to discipline, but it caused a considerable rift in the meantime. This is a topic they had never considered discussing, and their difference of opinions caught each of them off guard. This is a great example of having a conversation while things are calm before you are caught in the heat of the moment.

Outside Interests

You have (or had) a life prior to marriage. As a part of that you've participated in activities and established routines you enjoy and are comfortable with. While you may feel highly compatible with your partner, you are still two different people. What expectations do each of you share in terms of your time and attention?

- I expect to remain active in _____ (e.g. golf or bowling leagues, civic organizations, social clubs) once married.
- If yes, this would include _____ nights or hours per week.
- I expect to have regular evenings out with just my friends.
- If yes, how often?
- I can foresee us taking separate vacations.
- If yes, explain why.
- My career is critical to me. I will put in whatever hours are required over the long run to get ahead.
- I expect us to socialize together with friends on a regular basis.
- If yes, how often?
- I expect we will host friends and family at our home on a regular basis.
- If yes, who and how often?

These items should not be a surprise in marriage. If you don't discuss issues like these, you may assume your partner agrees with you in ways they don't. It's not disastrous to lack answers to these things in advance, but it can lead to frustration or disappointment.

Responsibilities

One of the first stumbling blocks that many newlyweds experience is when their spouse does not fulfill expectations. As a husband you may assume your wife is planning to cook most of the meals. As a wife you may think your husband can fix anything that breaks around the house. In reality you may both be wrong. She may only know how to cook one dish, and he may be mechanically inept. It is better to discuss these things before you are married than to be unpleasantly surprised afterwards.

It is important to note that the two of you were probably raised by families that divided up responsibilities differently. It could be that your dad paid all the bills and managed the bank accounts, but his mom did the same for his family. Therefore it is important you do not assume you and your spouse will divide up chores the same way your family did. This should not be a big deal, but it is important to have a discussion and agreement now to manage your mutual expectations later.

There may be some chores you enjoy and others you despise. You may be more gifted in some areas than others. Get this information out now so your marriage can start on a positive note. The following are areas to talk about and come to an agreement on. There will certainly be more, but these will get you started.

Which of you will…

- Shop for groceries?
- Cook?
- Do dishes?
- Clean the house?
- Maintain the cars?
- Do exterior work (e.g. mowing, landscaping, gardening, etc.)?
- Do laundry?
- Pay bills?
- Manage the family calendar?

Any of these tasks may be subdivided as you desire. As an example, you might clean up after a meal, and they might unload the dishwasher and put things away. You might plant flowers, and they might mow the lawn. The important thing is to determine who is doing what and not to falsely assume the other knows to do something you expect. The other key is to maintain flexibility in this area. If one of you is not feeling well, the other needs to step up and focus on their tasks in the short term. Don't fall into a "that's not my job" mentality. Agree on what needs to be done and develop a system to accomplish that.

Friends

Hopefully you've had a chance to meet and even interact with your partner's close network of friends by now. Ideally you have come to love them as if they were your own close friends, and your circle of close relationships has merely expanded. If that is the case, congratulations! But even if you have not, it is important to come to an understanding as to what role these people will play in your lives once you're married. It is important to manage expectations. You may have been in a Friday night poker game with your buddies for the past five years, but that doesn't mean your wife is willing to see you gone every weekend. Your wife now takes priority, and social scheduling is now done with the both of you. It doesn't mean you can never play again. She may want to do something with her friends occasionally on a Friday night also, in which case you both go out separately.

Extended Family

You are about to create a new, nuclear family. You are called to leave your current family and cleave with your partner. But that does not mean you sever all ties with the family that raised you. Your relationship with your parents, siblings, and others will change, but it should not evaporate. This is an area that causes tremendous stress in a lot of marriages, especially when it is not openly discussed and figured out in advance.

- What will the ongoing relationship with each set of parents look like?
- What are the expectations in terms of visiting?
- How will holidays be handled?

- Under what circumstances will advice be sought from either set of parents?
- Who will be included in our family gatherings?
- Under what circumstances will we bring both sides of the family together?
- Do you expect that your mom, dad, or both will live with you when they get older?
- What role do you see your families playing in the raising of your children?

Dealing with in-laws is often one of the first frustrations newly married couples face. The complexity of combining two (or more) extended families can be a daunting effort. Setting healthy boundaries and managing expectations is critical and should be done early on in the marriage. It is easier to relax boundaries later than it is to tighten them. It is impossible to realistically leave your family and cleave with your spouse if your relationship with your parents doesn't change. You must make it clear you are now part of something new to which you are giving priority. That doesn't mean you become rude or noncommunicative, but it is critical that your now extended family understands that your focus has shifted to your marriage. You are no longer under their control, their discipline, or their financial support. You are part of something new (and beautiful) that needs to stand on its own.

Managing In-laws

You've probably been told that when you marry the person, you marry their family as well. There is much truth in that. In-laws can literally be either a blessing or a curse to a marriage. Often times they are both. It is critical as a couple that you manage these expectations from the start. Like your marriage, these extended relationships will evolve over time. It is important to remain flexible and make adjustments as needed. But having some discussions on expectations from the start can reduce the potential volatility that may be experienced later.

You dated your spouse before you became engaged. There's a process we all go through during this time. We start out in a buying mode where we actively look for a person we feel will meet our needs over the long run. You may have dated several individuals before finding "the one" you wanted to go through life with. Once you decided they were the one for you, your efforts shifted from buying mode to selling mode. At this point you became determined to convince this person that you are the best option available to them. You wanted to outshine and outperform all others they might consider. At some point you made the joint decision to pursue marriage.

What's interesting is that the in-laws go through a similar process. They may express some curiosity about who their child is dating but typically won't invest in creating a relationship until they sense that something serious is taking place. At that point they also go into sales mode, putting forward their best efforts and attitudes to make a great impression. You typically don't see flaws at this point; they are well-hidden behind carefully constructed facades. But these facades wear down over time. Depending on the length of your relationship and engagement, you may or may not see the real nature of your spouse's parents prior to marriage. Your fiancé may attempt to forewarn you about certain proclivities regarding their parents, or they may be oblivious to them. It is important to remember that what may seem odd to you is what they have been raised with.

In time everybody lets their guard down and becomes their natural selves. You may find this endearing or annoying. Either way you'll need to learn to live with and manage the relationship. A classic example illustrating this would be the manner in which you address your in-laws. It could start out very formally as in Mr. and Mrs. Jones. As the relationship grows, they may invite you to call them by their first names, Ed and Sally. In some cases you may even begin to call them Mom and Dad, or once you have kids, Grandma and Grandpa. The point is that the relationship will evolve over time. With some proactive effort, you can grow closer and feel as if you have added to your family in a blessed manner.

You know the relationship your partner has with his or her parents and siblings. They may be very close, or the relationship might be strained. You will develop some sense of how well they accept you. The key is to understand how that relationship will impact your marriage. I have seen a few situations where the in-laws were instrumental in eroding a marriage to the point of collapse. An extreme example of this is shown below.

John was a European living in his home country of France. He met Sue, an American expatriate working in his hometown. They began dating and soon fell in love. He proposed to her, and they were married within months. What John didn't realize was the tight bond that existed between Sue and her parents. Sue came from a very wealthy family that had provided her with the best of everything her whole life. Her father provided her with and paid for an exclusive credit card with no spending limit. She could go anywhere and do anything with no concern for budget.

Unfortunately, Sue's father did not approve of the marriage. From his perspective John did not run in the proper social circles or come from the type of family worthy of his daughter. From the start he tried to convince his daughter that she had made a mistake and needed to leave her husband. John was committed to the marriage, but Sue did not sever ties with her family. The father rescinded the credit card and cut her off from the lifestyle she had grown accustomed to. To make things worse, the father continued to tell Sue about the benefits she would regain if only she would come to her senses and leave John.

John worked hard to provide Sue with what he could, but there was no way he could compete with the resources her father had at his disposal. I believe Sue could have been content with what she had with John if her father was not constantly in her ear, planting seeds of discontent. Sadly, the marriage dissolved within the first year. She was immediately rewarded by getting her credit card back. John was devastated.

It's clear that John and Sue did not have sufficient discussions on this topic prior to their marriage. John assumed they would start their own lives together, and Sue never really considered her life without the benefits she'd always enjoyed. This was not a couple of faith, so they were not able to call God into the equation to intervene. But it's clear that a lack of understanding, discussion, and planning led to this tragedy.

While this was an extreme example, I can't think of a couple that hasn't experienced some level of tension surrounding their in-laws. It is important to establish boundaries early on and to manage expectations with all involved. It is easier to ease up on boundaries down the road than it is to implement them once routines have been established.

From time to time you and your spouse will have conflicts. Be very cautious about venting or complaining about your spouse to your parents. When you do this, you are essentially trying to create a division on an issue and get your parents on your side, opposing your spouse. The odds are they will empathize with you. That may feel good in the moment, but it has significantly detrimental effects down the road. Inevitably you will walk away from the conversation and go back to your marriage. You make up with your spouse, and everything is much better. With your frustration abated, it doesn't occur to you to update your parents on your reconciliation. Essentially you have planted seeds of distrust and anger in them towards your spouse. The next time you all sit down together for dinner, you may not realize why the mood is so tense. You moved on, but your parents haven't had the chance.

Likewise, be careful in complaining about your in-laws to your parents. Just as it did with your spouse, this creates feelings of dislike or mistrust between your two sets of parents. When I was first married, I didn't always like the way my father-in-law treated his daughter (my wife, Tara). I know Tara didn't like some of his attitudes or behavior either. But I made the mistake of sharing with my mom some of these frustrations. She then took it upon herself to dislike my father-in-law and make the assumption that Tara must not like him either. She would then proceed to make some pretty brash comments to Tara about her dad, and frankly that was not okay. This in turn led to significant stress between Tara and I that never really needed to happen.

There may be a time and a place to seek wisdom and advice from your parents regarding your marriage, but the request needs to be carefully pursued. Instead of complaining about your spouse to them, you could ask them questions such as "Did you ever go through a season where you felt you weren't truly appreciated by Dad?" or "How did you and Mom come to an agreement when you were on opposite sides of an issue?" Asking in this way invites advice without assigning blame. It's a way to learn from a couple you trust without forcing them to take sides. Remember, you never want to intentionally drive a wedge between yourself and your spouse. And you especially don't want to invite your parents to be part of that wedge.

In addition to your mother-in-law and father-in-law, it is important to address any other extended family members that may have direct interaction with your marriage. What is the relationship that you each have with your grandparents? Your siblings? What expectations exist with these family members? These relationships won't necessarily cause stress, but it's important to talk about any preexisting expectations. Perhaps you have an aging grandmother that you are especially close to. You currently see her every week, and you hope to continue doing so after you are married. There is nothing wrong with that. It's simply important to let your spouse know so that you can manage expectations. You may have a special needs sibling you have agreed to care for if anything ever happens to your parents. Be it a formal obligation or merely an implied understanding, I recommend you discuss these assumptions with each other prior to marriage.

Adult relationships with parents vary widely. For some, parents are close confidantes and are spoken to daily. For others it's strictly cordial, and for some it may be a strained or distant relationship. The important thing is not to assume the relationship you have with your parents is the same your partner has with theirs. Talk openly about how each of you feels about and interacts with your parents on an ongoing basis.

While I remember navigating these waters with my in-laws nearly forty years ago, I've since been through the experience (from the in-law's perspective) with my two older sons. Both of my sons married girls from great Christian families. To make things easier, both of their families lived in the same area as us. On the surface you would think this integration process would have been very simple. In both cases it was not, and it caused considerable stress as my sons and their wives tried to manage expectations on both sides of their family. As newlywed couples their goal was to make everybody happy and to attempt to meet all parents' expectations. Their first objective was to divide everything (time, attention, spending, etc.) evenly over two sides of the family. "If we spend a full day and have dinner with your family, we'll have to find another full day including dinner to spend with mine." That may work out fine most of the time, but what happens when you enter into the holiday season? Which family gets Christmas or Thanksgiving Day proper as opposed to an alternate day? This same attitude carried on throughout the year. "We went out to dinner with your parents twice last month, we have to go out now twice with mine." The effort to balance was trying and exhausting.

What's funny is that many of these decisions were made without consulting either set of parents. While the parents were similar in many ways, many subtle differences allowed things to be worked out. Firstly, both couples took Christmas Day off the table, saying they wanted to begin their own family traditions—spending it together. Once neither set of parents was competing to host Christmas Day, they became willing to compromise to enjoy time on another (near to Christmas) day. Problem solved. In terms of the other events, they both tried to honor unique days of importance (birthday celebrations, significant sibling events, etc.) but didn't worry about keeping things exactly even. They learned how to interact with each family positively in a way their parents most appreciated.

It would be far better to think through and have these conversations before you are confronted with them. Taking a proactive approach allows you to have a broader perspective and consider more options. When you are forced to make a choice on the spot, you may not choose the wisest option. As an example, talking about Christmas plans before they are set in stone and discussing alternatives can lead to less stress than approaching the date only to find everyone is expecting you to be at a given place at a predetermined time. You will never be able to please everyone completely, but understanding desires and communicating plans in advance can go a long way toward avoiding conflict with extended family.

Perhaps you and your spouse will live in the same area your parents do. Dividing time equally in this situation is relatively easy in that you can see either family on short notice. You can be there as things arise, and you can count on them to help you when you are in need. This becomes especially helpful once you have children. Having grandparents nearby can greatly ease the stress associated with finding a babysitter. On the flip side it can be harder to manage expectations. Because of your proximity it may be assumed that you are available to attend every event or help out in any situation. In these cases it will be important to establish some guidelines as to what you will and won't participate in. You will have to maintain the priority on your new relationship and not let yourselves get sucked back into your extended families.

You may not even be living in the same state as either of your parents. In some ways this makes planning easier because no one can expect you to be in two places on the same day. However, this situation forces you to do more advanced planning and negotiating. How you resolve this will be up to you. Some couples rotate holidays (Thanksgiving with his parents, Christmas with hers) and others rotate years (Christmas with his family this year, her family next). That's not ideal for anyone, but there may be no other realistic options available.

When Tara and I first married, we moved about five hours away from our hometown where both of our parents still lived. When we would come home for holidays or vacation, we would alternate parents to stay with but drive to the other's home to spend time there as well. Over time we all came to realize that it was more comfortable for everyone involved for us to stay at my parent's (larger) home at night but spend comparable time during the day at Tara's family.

You may be facing a completely different situation. You could be living near one set of parents and far from the other. You might both be products of divorced families, giving you multiple sets of parents and in-laws to manage. The point here is not to provide a specific solution but rather to stress the importance of discussing situations in advance and communicating the plan with all parties involved. There may be some disappointment expressed initially, but you ultimately have to do what is best for you as a couple while satisfying extended family as best as possible.

Be forewarned. As complex as managing all this sounds when you are first married, it gets exponentially harder once you have kids. It's a funny thing. Parents seem to be able to go without seeing their kids for a while, but deprive them of time with their grandkids…watch out!

Summary

Hopefully you can see and appreciate the point of this chapter. Spending time talking with your partner about life experiences, preferences, dislikes, and habits can go a long way guiding you toward a smooth future. So often when couples are dating, tough or awkward conversations are avoided. It's far more fun to focus on fun and romance than to get into unpleasant topics. Unless you are marrying a clone of yourself, you will never be completely aligned on every topic or past experience. Thank God for the unique person He has brought into your life. In time you can learn to appreciate and utilize the diversity of perspective your future spouse brings to you. Managing expectations in advance can eliminate a lot of headaches.

Discussion Questions

1. Under the heading "Cast a Vision for your Marriage" it is suggested that you cast a vision for yourself before your marriage. Now is a good time to do so. Don't rush it! Be as thorough as you can be. Consider going away for a day of contemplation to get yourself started. Consider journaling the process.

2. Consider the story of Joe and Sue and discuss it with your fiancé. Does the possibility of working through a process of combining your lives in this way excite you, scare you? What emotions come to the front?

3. Now would be a good time to sit down with your future spouse and answer some of the questions listed in this chapter. You are encouraged to take some time away from each other and then come together to carefully share your heart. Write your answers down as completely as you can.

CHAPTER 5
MERGING LIVES -
LEARN THE WORD "OURS"

Preparing for marriage is an exciting time. You begin planning your future together, sharing your dreams and your expectations. Children, careers, desired home styles and future vacations are all topics readily discussed. While it may be easy to share dreams, it's harder to take time to consider things that might have to be given up for the sake of the relationship. Budgets, schedules, and priorities are all areas that need to be managed as a couple. The longer you have lived on your own and created your own lifestyle and habits, the harder it may be to merge your lifestyle with your new spouse. As you've already read, two people becoming one flesh includes two separate people growing to share one life. To truly experience the blessings that come with being one flesh, it is important you begin to look at life from a joint perspective, not from a selfish one. The word *ours* should become more significant to you than the word *mine*.

Creating the "Ours" Mentality

The concept of your things becoming our things may come easily to you, or it may be difficult. Your attitude stems from a multitude of different factors. If you were an only child, you didn't have to share your things or time with others. On the other hand, if you had multiple siblings, you may have had very few things you could actually call your own as most things were shared. You may have been raised in a home where money was tight and possessions were sparse, and when you did get something special, you held onto it with all your might. You may have come from a home where resources were abundant, possessions came easily, and very little was highly valued.

The model you witnessed growing up has a huge impact on your attitude as well. Did your parents share an "ours" mentality, or did they each have their own things and plan their own time? Perhaps you witnessed your parents divorcing and saw an ugly side of "that's mine" emerge as your household was divided.

No matter where you fall on the above examples, the odds are your future spouse was raised in a different situation. Creating an ours mentality will take intentional effort and a lot of conversation. The first thing to realize is that it's not about giving up things but rather about sharing things with your one-flesh partner. But it also doesn't mean you are giving up your identity, your passions, or your desires. You will remain two unique people even as you become one flesh.

When Tara and I were first married, we were still in college and living in married student apartments. In those days video arcades were a big thing, and I loved to meet my buddies there to play such epic games as Pac-Man, Ms. Pac-Man, and Galaga. One day I got a call from a friend asking me to meet him at the arcade. I looked around the apartment for any loose change but could find none. I started looking through drawers and happened to find a few roles of quarters with Tara's things. Bingo! One role would be enough for forty games; I was set. I saw no issue in this. After all, we were married, so her things were my things.

When I returned home later that afternoon, I told Tara where I'd been. She casually asked me where I'd gotten the money from, and I told her about my find. She exploded with rage. "What's the big deal?" I asked. "I'll give you back ten dollars." She went on to tell me those were special quarters her coin-collecting grandfather had given her. Each coin had something unique about it that made it worth more than twenty-five cents. These were something special she was holding onto both from a sentimental and an investment standpoint. Oops. The key here is to understand that the ours mentality requires not only trust but also respect. Ideally she would have told me these quarters were special. But I had no business taking them out of her drawer without first asking.

Just because something is ours does not mean either person has the right to do with it whatever they want. There is a bit of a balancing act required here. You will have some things you value that your spouse has no interest in and vice versa. It is important you respect these items and their opinion and don't assume value based on your opinion alone. I've seen tremendous hurt occur in marriages when one spouse discards or sells an item that was important to the other, assuming it was no longer needed. "Ours" may give you a say in a situation but not necessarily the final say.

In a similar vein, when two individuals marry and come to establish a common household, negotiation and compromise become important ingredients in the relationship. He may want to continue to proudly display the deer head from his first hunt on the wall above the fireplace. She may be appalled at that thought. Conversely, she might have a very particular style in which she wants to decorate. It might not be his taste. How do you reconcile these differences?

It is important to realize you are establishing your home together. You both need to feel like you have a say in the decisions and are able to come to an agreement on what the eventual look is. Sometimes the husband doesn't care and encourages his wife to decorate as she desires. Other times the couple will divide up areas or rooms of the house. He has his man cave and may style it as he wishes, and she has the rest of the house. The key is not to assume one solution or another without first having a conversation. You both want to be comfortable in your home, and neither of you should feel like you've sold out in what it looks like.

Answer these questions individually. Then discuss as a couple:

- Is it easy or hard for me to share my possessions?
- How much control do I need when laying out or decorating my house?

Money

One of the first areas facing newly married couples is money—how it is earned, saved, spent, and invested. While this was a relatively simple process as a single adult, you will begin to face each decision with two opinions instead of one. Being aligned in financial philosophy and planning is important. It will require an ongoing effort to get there, but doing so will save you a tremendous amount of grief over time. While planning your marriage, have an open and transparent discussion about your individual attitudes toward money.

A 2017 Magnify Money survey[9] of five hundred divorced US adults found twenty-one percent of divorcees cited money as the cause of their divorce. For younger couples aged twenty-five to forty-four years old, the statistics were even higher at twenty-four percent. Discrepancies regarding money is in fact one of the leading causes of divorce. In most cases overspending by one partner or the other was the leading contributor. Lying about spending was prevalent as well. It would appear in these cases that couples never came together on this topic but rather attempted to maintain the lifestyle and decision-making process they had enjoyed as a single person.

When it comes to budgeting, spending, and saving, you are a product of your upbringing. The views your family had on

---

[9] Magnify Money 2017 "Divorce and Debt Survey" February 13, 2017

money have influenced and shaped the person you are today, and you and your fiancé were raised with different experiences. It is unrealistic to think the two of you can come together and meld your financial philosophies with no stress or disagreement.

Heather and Colin came into their marriage from opposite ends of the financial spectrum. Colin had attended a prestigious University on a full ride scholarship and parlayed that into a very successful business career. Heather was a single mom who had to make every penny count. She knew where the lowest prices were on any home item one could imagine. When they married, they had to come to an agreement about the new reality they found themselves in. Fortunately, they learned the fine art of mutual submission and came up with a solution reflective of both their life experiences. They are happily married to this day.

As a single person you have developed a financial lifestyle you are comfortable with. You may not think twice about dropping a hundred and fifty dollars for a round of golf or spending a hundred dollars on a hair appointment. After all, it's your money, you've earned it, and it is fully within your rights to determine how to spend it.

That may have been true when you lived alone, but that part of your life is about to change. You may hear secular financial advisors recommend you maintain separate bank accounts once you've wed. This protects your rights to "spend as you please" with no pressure or guilt. This flies in the face of the type of relationship God intends for you to have in marriage. It makes no sense to be one flesh but have separate means of financial sustenance. Becoming one with your partner means thriving together in good times and struggling together when times are tough financially. I've heard some men sarcastically say, "What's hers is hers, and what's mine is ours…" While they were joking, there is some frustration expressed in their statement. There should be no yours, mine, and ours—simply ours. This takes considerable transparency, trust, and communication.

I know married couples that have chosen to keep their money separate. Sometimes they maintain individual accounts and open an additional joint account. In these cases they divide up the bills based on how much each partner earns. As an example, if she makes one hundred thousand dollars per year and he makes fifty thousand dollars, she would pay two thirds of the mortgage payment, and he would pay one third. This allocation approach would apply to all ongoing bills. Whatever each partner has in their account after the bills have been paid can be spent as they individually choose.

This may seem like a fair and logical way of dividing up the household budget, but having individual spending limits based upon earning is a slippery slope. What happens if you decide one of you will continue to work while the other stays home to raise the children? Which of you is adding the most value to the family at that point? I have seen couples in this situation where the stay-at-home spouse begins to feel trapped. Because they are not earning a wage, they feel subordinate to the working spouse and may even tolerate situations they shouldn't have to.

It is not imperative you and your spouse are identical in your views toward money. In fact, God often delights in bringing together a spender and a saver. There are strengths and benefits to both types of people, and when they learn to work together, it benefits the marriage as a whole. It is important that you are open with your spouse about your habits and preferences but even more important that you are willing to adjust your habits for the good of the relationship. Putting together a financial plan for the two of you is a critical first step toward this upcoming transition.

Before you get to the altar to say "I do," you need to talk openly about money. This is a time to lay it all out on the table, hiding nothing. You may be embarrassed you have accumulated ten thousand dollars in credit card debt or eighty thousand dollars in unpaid college loans, but it is far better to talk about this before your wedding than to find out about it upon returning from your honeymoon. Likewise, you may have a history of overspending, resulting in a low credit score. Sharing this fact with your partner now allows you to develop a collaborative plan to rectify it. You don't want this to surface when you are jointly applying for your first mortgage. Being declined for that reason would not only be humiliating, but it would leave you no time to make alternative plans. Once you marry, your assets and liabilities become jointly owned. Therefore it is imperative you agree on how your money will be handled.

Answer these questions individually, then discuss them as a couple:

- In terms of money, am I more of a spender or a saver? Give examples.
- Am I comfortable with the concept of combining our money into a joint account? Why or why not?
- What assets do I bring into the marriage?
- What debts do I bring into the marriage?

Creating a Budget

A Career Builder poll conducted in 2017[10] found seventy-eight percent of Americans live paycheck to paycheck. If you were to ask most couples what causes this, they would tell you they don't earn enough. In their minds, if they could only increase their incomes by fifteen to twenty percent, they would be in great shape and could begin saving significant money. Ironically, according to a 2015 Nielsen study[11], twenty-five percent of Americans earning over one hundred and fifty thousand dollars are also living paycheck to paycheck. It would appear the mere act of earning more money does not solve the problem.

Many couples look at their income and then figure out how they can spend up to that amount. They buy the biggest home the bank tells them they can afford. They furnish it, taking advantage of "twelve months same as cash" financing deals.

---

[10] "Living Paycheck to Paycheck is a way of Life…" Career Builder August 24, 2017
[11] "Saving, Spending and Living Paycheck to Paycheck…" Nielson July 28, 2015

They buy new cars with five-year loans. Before long there's no decisions to be made because every dollar is spoken for. When unexpected expenses arise, they cover them with a credit card. These couples are not only living paycheck to paycheck. They may be making ridiculously high interest-only payments on their credit cards. Living like this will generate considerable stress in your marriage.

As previously stated, there are many different attitudes toward money, saving, and spending. As a single person you may know where you spent every penny, or you may have started a budget but never followed through with it. Perhaps you never had a budget at all. You had only yourself to answer to. When it comes to household budgets, the old saying is very applicable: "Failing to plan is planning to fail." This will not be the most fun conversation you have when planning your marriage, but it may be one of the most critical. Too many assume they will simply figure this out as they go, and before long find themselves in a financial bind. It is much easier to create a plan you implemented from the start than it is to figure out how to get out of a horrible debt situation later.

Create a budget as a couple. As believers one of the first things to understand about money is that it all belongs to God. We have been called to be good stewards of the share with which He has blessed us. A big part of good stewardship is giving to God from our first fruits.

> "Honor the Lord with your wealth, with the firstfruits of all your crops; then your barns will be filled to overflowing, and your vats will brim over with new wine."
>
> —Proverbs 3:9-10 NIV

For too many this concept is reversed in their lives. They pay all their bills, then buy things they desire. At the end of the month, if there is any money left, they donate a portion to the church. That's like giving your scraps to God, the opposite of what we are called to do. You may wonder, how could we possibly give to church before we know how much we have available after paying bills and other expenses?

> Bring all the tithes into the storehouse so there will be enough food in my Temple. "If you do," says the Lord of Heaven's Armies, "I will open the windows of heaven for you. I will pour out a blessing so great you won't have enough room to take it in! Try it! Put me to the test!"
>
> —Malachi 3:10 NLT

God has a plan for that. This is the only passage in the Bible where God encourages us to challenge Him. Tithing can be a frightening concept for many couples. As you look at the resources you have, you may be thinking you barely have enough to get by. How could you possibly get by with ten percent less? That's where faith comes in. If you and your spouse prayerfully agree to tithe, the Bible promises God will take care of you. It doesn't say specifically how, but it assures He will.

If you are taking your one-flesh covenant relationship with God seriously, this is a tremendous way to include Him in a very tangible way. Think of it this way: if everything truly belongs to God, He is letting you keep ninety percent of what is rightfully His. Give to Him from your first fruits.

Start out by identifying your collective debt. Student loans, car payments, and credit card debt should all be shared. If you both have these liabilities, it will feel pretty overwhelming when you see them combined. On one hand it might provide some relief to think your burdens will now be shared with another. On the other hand you may be gaining some debt you hadn't considered. Remember, you are marrying the whole person, including their assets and liabilities. You can't put together a realistic plan until you see the big picture for what it truly is.

Identifying and discussing debt does not make it more real or more frightening. Debt exists whether you acknowledge it or not. Openly discussing it is the only way to create a proactive plan moving forward. Nothing should be hidden at this point;

ignorance is not bliss in this area. Once you've done this, you know what lies ahead of you in terms of planning.

Next, take a look at your combined income as a couple. In a one-flesh relationship, it doesn't matter if one partner is contributing more financially to the marriage than the other. It's not like buying stock in a company. In that scenario, the more money you put in, the more influence you have in how things are run. You don't become one flesh with other stockholders. Now you can see the total money coming in and the debt that has to be repaid. It is time to identify all of the ongoing, fixed costs you will have as a couple. This should include your rent or mortgage payments, utilities, and other such expenses.

The next area would be ongoing costs you have some control over. As an example, you need to plan for food and groceries. As you develop the budget, you can begin to see the difference in cost between eating out and eating in. You also have some control over the cost of the groceries you procure. You may have only eaten name brand items while single, but it may be time to switch to generics until some of your debt is paid off.

Most financial experts strongly recommend a couple has a three-to-six-month emergency fund set aside. These would be funds readily available in case of job loss, medical issues, or major car repairs. As you begin planning your budget with your spouse, it is critical you allow for such an account to be established and funded. When you make your wedding vows, you may say things like "for better or worse, for richer or poorer…" In reality most couples go through tough times over the course of their marriage. Those financially prepared for such events undergo far less stress than those that have to make sudden, drastic decisions in order to stay afloat.

Your emergency fund won't emerge overnight. It is critical you allocate money in your budget to create this. It may take a year or longer to achieve this. Once the fund is fully established, you can reallocate that line item to another account. Financially conservative couples will shift that money toward retirement. Others may sock it away for a dream vacation. Whatever decision you make, make it together.

Once you have planned for ongoing and fixed expenses, you should plan how you will allocate the money remaining each month. The focus of this chapter is not to help you develop a comprehensive financial strategy but rather to gain alignment between you and your spouse on creating a plan. While it is easy to agree on (but not necessarily simple to execute) the basics, discretionary income is where you will need to have real discussion and negotiation. You are likely to find there is not enough money remaining for each of you to continue to enjoy the spending you had when living alone. So, who is going to compromise, and on what? Once you are married, planning for the future will take on a new level of importance. Be it saving for the down payment on a house, planning for a family, or investing for retirement, your savings won't build unless you consciously put money aside.

It is important that each spouse has some agreed upon level of autonomy in their spending. Dave Ramsey in his financial planning materials calls this blow money[12]: money set aside for each person that can be spent with no justification or permission. This becomes a line item in the couple's budget. This amount can change over time as the couple's income increases or decreases or as debt is reduced.

When Tara and I first started out, I was working full time, and she was working part time as she completed her college degree. We didn't have a rigid budget, but we had a strong sense of where our money was going. At that time we agreed we could each spend up to fifty dollars per month with no guilt or discussion. That worked well for us. Fast forward ten years and my income had risen considerably. We had two young kids and jointly made the decision Tara would leave her job to stay home with them. In spite of that we decided at that time our individual discretionary funds could rise to two hundred and fifty dollars per month. Fast forward another ten years and I left the security of my corporate job to start my own business. With the uncertainty of income stemming from a

---

[12] DaveRamsey.com "What is Blow Money For?"

new business, our monthly allotment dropped back down to a hundred dollars each.

The point is not the specific dollar amount but rather the discussion and agreement to abide by a number that works for each of you. It's unrealistic to say every dollar spent must be jointly agreed upon or preapproved. But having no limit at all will lead you into mounting debt that can eventually bury you.

Answer these questions individually, then discuss them as a couple:

- Do I live by a strict budget or a loose budget, or do I have no budget at all?
- Am I comfortable with the idea of creating a combined household budget?
- What is my attitude and history of church giving?
- How have I dealt with unplanned or emergency financial issues in the past?

Joint Schedules

It's not only important to budget your money as a couple but also your time. As a single person you determine not only your own spending habits but also your own schedule. You probably spend considerable time with your partner but still have available time to schedule as you wish.

You do not need to plan to spend every moment together as a married couple; that would be unhealthy. But you will have another person to consider in your scheduling moving forward. The key is to be aware and considerate. These days most people plan their lives on their smart phones. It is important when you pull up your calendar that you see not only your schedule but that of your spouse as well. This will allow you to make better decisions with your time. If you are both working, a large part of your individual schedules will be out of your control. Be it business travel or overtime, you may find you are away from each other more than you would like to be. That only makes it more important that you jointly plan the available time you do have together. Plan something in the evenings when you see your spouse is busy and try to be home when they're home. This simple trick will go a long way toward enabling you to spend quality time together.

Blending Families

This may not be your first marriage or your fiancé's. If that is the case, you may be bringing kids into the marriage from day one. You may have sole or primary custody, or you may only have your kids every other weekend and on alternating holidays. Regardless, this is a big issue you need to manage from the start.

This situation brings even greater importance to the shared schedule concept discussed earlier. You need to have a clear understanding of who is going to be in your house and when. This becomes considerably more complex because you are dealing with additional family units. As a blended family the parenting schedule won't always allow your kids to be with you for special events or holidays. It is important you work with your ex to make these dates work out as best as possible for all involved. Showing your kids you can be flexible and communicate with their other parent will speak volumes.

Beyond scheduling, blended families face a variety of unique issues. In some cases not only are you getting remarried, but your ex (and their ex) may have also remarried. It is very unlikely you will get up to six individuals perfectly aligned in terms of boundaries and parenting philosophies. Your kids will need to understand that they live by different rules when in different homes. If you are becoming a stepparent through this marriage, it is important you work with your partner's children. Let them know you are not trying to replace their mom or dad, but you are there to love and support them in everything they do.

As a couple you will need to discuss and agree on the upcoming role of the stepparent. Do they have authority to advise or discipline children who are not biologically their own? Are they expected to treat the kids differently than you do? If they also have kids, will they treat your kids differently from their own? Working through these issues prior to marriage can save you a lot of grief and frustration later.

One issue commonly seen in blended family situations is the desire to protect children from further emotional damage. There is typically a tremendous amount of guilt carried by the biological parent for having put their children through the dissolution of their original family. These feelings create a desire to shield kids from any further risk of disruption. This can essentially result in the creation of multiple, independent families living under the same roof. You have husband and wife, Mom with her kids, and Dad with his—each family living under different rules and expectations. This may be inevitable to some degree, but strive to create a sense of one family within your household.

Children are often more adaptable than they are given credit for. In time they can come to understand they exist as a part of multiple family units. When they're with Dad, they have one family with a given structure and a given set of rules, and when they're with Mom, they are part of a different family. When a biological parent excludes the stepparent from being a part of the child's life, they risk sending the message that the new marriage is transient. They communicate that the child is the most important relationship in their life and their new spouse is secondary. This is not a good model to show or teach children. In fact, it can encourage older children to play their biological parent against their spouse in an unhealthy manner.

Your children are watching you. They are looking for the behaviors and patterns they saw in your previous marriage. In their minds, they may expect your current marriage to fall apart much like your last one did. In some cases, that may be their desire. They want you to "get over" this new person so you will go back to your former spouse, and then life will be as it was before your divorce. It is critical to express to them that this marriage is not temporary and is in fact committed to God. Over time they will see the difference between what you have now and what you had before. Be aware of this and be very conscientious about the marriage you are modeling.

Co-parenting is often not easy. You may find yourself living in a very different environment than your ex. You may not agree on fundamental issues regarding their upbringing. As a result, your kids may be subjected to radically different values or rules when they go from your home to theirs. There may be nothing about your ex's home you can influence or control, but it is critical you and your new spouse are on the same page regarding how things will be in your home. You will need to spend significant time discussing this as a couple both up front and on an ongoing basis. There is no way you could possibly anticipate every situation that will arise. But the more you are philosophically aligned, the better you will do as a couple and as parents.

In protecting your marriage, it is important you share what is going on with your ex and with your kids. It is not fair for you to unexpectedly erupt at your spouse because you had a conflict with your ex earlier in the day. It is important to understand the relationship your kids have with their other biological parent and to communicate with your spouse as well. The goal is to remain on the same page, talk through trying issues, and create a plan that works as well as possible.

Merging Interests

You and your partner have come to learn you have much in common. It is these shared interests in part that have brought you to the point of planning marriage. It is important to note, however, that you will also have independent interests that are of little to no appeal to each other. Some of these differences might dissipate, but others you will need to learn to accommodate and support. If you keep an open mind, you may learn to love and share new interests based on your spouse's passions.

Mike and Susan met at a State University, fell in love, and married. Before they married, it was clear Susan had a huge passion for orphans in other countries; it was a regular topic of conversation. Sometime after their wedding it was easy to see Susan's passion for orphans had become Mike's passion as well. Their refrigerator was completely covered with Compassion Children, their recreation time included serving at Feed My Starving Children, and vacations included visiting orphanages in Africa.

It might be a hobby you come to share an interest in. I know one couple where the wife decided to learn about football because she knew that was important to her husband. Fast forward a few years and they have season tickets to their local pro team and enjoy spending their Sunday afternoons together cheering at the stadium.

If you find there are areas of interest not shared, have a discussion and come to an understanding regarding them. The key is to keep a healthy balance in the relationship. It's okay if he loves to watch sports on television. But if he is dominating the television every night, then it becomes a problem. I've heard wives describe themselves as "sports widows." Never neglect your spouse on an ongoing basis because of your outside interests or hobbies.

Friends can fall into this same category. Prior to marriage you probably had your friends, and your partner had theirs. Ideally these individuals become your collective friends, but that doesn't always happen. Just as with hobbies and interests, it is fine to have the occasional girls or guys night out, but those should be scheduled in such a way as to minimize the effect on the marriage.

Answer these questions individually, then discuss them as a couple:

- What interests do we share as a couple?
- What unique interests do we have that are not shared?
- How willing am I to gain interest in my spouse's unique interests?

Summary

Once you are married, you will have two sets of ideas and opinions to deal with. In a one-flesh relationship, you will share assets and liabilities, calendars, and friends. Some of these mergers will happen easily, but others will require effort on both of your parts. The key is to understand that there is another person coming into your life, and you both need to operate from a perspective of "ours."

Discussion Questions

1. Follow the instruction in this chapter and identify your collective debt.
2. Calculate your combined income as a couple.
3. Identify all of the ongoing, fixed costs you will have as a couple, including the accumulation of an emergency fund.
4. Identify hobbies and passions that each of you have as individuals. Discuss how those might play out once you are married.
5. Are you forming a blended family? Consider meeting with a well-established Christian family that is blended for insights.

PART 3
TIPS TO SUSTAINING A SHOCKING MARRIAGE

CHAPTER 6
INTIMACY - START HOT, STAY HOT

If you have held off on having sex before marriage—congratulations! You must be excited about the discovery, pleasure, and long-awaited fulfillment that lies ahead. I (Jerry) recently did premarital counseling for a young couple. They are both strong believers and committed to abstaining from sex prior to marriage. Through our conversations it was obvious they were both excited about having sex, and the anticipation was growing exponentially over the weeks we met. Their wedding was beautiful; it was one of the most sexually charged ceremonies I have ever attended (in a beautiful and tasteful manner). They couldn't keep their hands off of each other and never once hesitated when prompted to kiss. They went to a tropical island for their honeymoon and posted pictures on social media. The look in their eyes spoke volumes of the passion and love they were sharing together. That is the way God intended it to be. Sexual discovery should occur after the wedding when there is no guilt, no regret, and no insecurity. Anticipation is the ultimate foreplay.

You may be thinking, "But we didn't wait—we have been sexually active. What about us?" The reality is that when separated from the lifelong commitment of marriage, sex will never bring the satisfaction God designed it to give. Sex outside of marriage is sin, and sin always hinders intimacy. But sin can be forgiven through the grace of Jesus Christ. If you want your married sex life to be blessed, then put it on hold until you are wed. Seek forgiveness and wait until you enter into a covenant relationship (your wedding) before you resume having sex. You will not experience the blessing of your first time together as originally intended, but you can still have a fantastic, God-blessed sex life moving forward.

Regardless of where you've been, let's shift the focus to where you want to head. Thousands of books have been written on the topics of intimacy and sexuality. Amazon lists over one hundred titles focused specifically on intimacy and sexuality for Christian marriage alone. In addition, hundreds of blogs and podcasts are focused on this clearly important topic. Intimacy is a huge source of conflict in a marriage. In a covenant, one-flesh relationship, this should not be the case, so why is there so much frustration?

Many people, especially men, focus on sex to determine personal and marital satisfaction. In their minds, frequent and exciting sex signifies a great relationship. Infrequent, mediocre sex suggests the marriage is subpar at best. In reality sexual union is always more than merely physical. There is relational and emotional oneness as well. Most sexual issues in marriage stem from a failure of experiencing or providing total-person intimacy. God designed us in such a way that sexual harmony must be built on the foundation of a primary, permanent, exclusive relationship growing in trust, openness, and oneness. Sex is a key component of a great marriage. If you remove sex from marriage, you will experience a superficial sense of closeness akin to living with a friend as a roommate. But having a great sex life without an intimate relationship is highly unlikely.

Defining Intimacy

Let's take a look at the relationship between sex and intimacy. To most men the words *sex* and *intimacy* are synonymous. But for women these are two very different topics sharing some overlap. While sex may be a component of intimacy for women, it is typically not the primary driver.

You may never understand this concept the same way your spouse does, but knowing you perceive intimacy differently is important. With knowledge comes understanding, and understanding leads to deeper relationship. In this chapter you will see God's perspective and develop keys to bridge any intimacy gaps existing in your relationship.

It took me (Jerry) several years of marriage to understand these differences in perception. When Tara and I began leading marriage workshops through our church, we put together a multisession agenda with each week focused on a different topic. The final capstone meeting dealt with sex. After all, once couples mastered topics such as building a foundation on Christ or dealing with conflict, finances, and communication, they'd be ready to shift their focus to the ultimate goal and learn how to enhance their sex life.

After offering our workshops three or four times, Tara asked me, "Why do we sequence our topics like we do; specifically, why do we offer the sex module at the end?" At first, I thought she was kidding. To me the order of our workshop was obvious, each session building on the previous one and climaxing (pardon the pun) with sex. She suggested we move the module on communication to the end. In her mind, sex was important but only a step along the path, not the finish line. Talk about an eye-opener! This led to further discussion that really opened my eyes to her perspective. Once I overcame my paradigm, I came to understand she was not alone in her thinking among females.

Jimmy Evans, founder of Marriage Today[13], speaks about the greatest needs of men and women in marriage:

Husbands' greatest needs:

1. Honor and respect
2. Sexual intimacy
3. Friendship (with their spouse)

Wives' greatest needs:

1. Security
2. Non-sexual affection
3. Open and honest communication

These lists explain the differences in priority that Tara and I were expressing. A fantastic sex life is high on the men's list and is something to continually strive for. But for wives sex doesn't even make the top three needs.

Women inherently grasp intimacy is a multifaceted topic. God did not create marriage with the intent of frustrating couples. Rather, he created us to have different but complementary desires that should be *mutually fulfilled*. Before you can improve the intimacy in your marriage, it is critical to create a common understanding on what the concept means for both you and your spouse.

Dictionary.com defines intimacy as "a close, familiar, and usually affectionate or loving personal relationship with another person." Most couples could agree on this definition, but it is still open to much interpretation. Guys would still think primarily of sex, and women would see it as considerably more, expanding into areas like transparency and emotional connectedness. Neither are wrong. Intimacy needs to be understood as a broad and diverse topic. It's the glue that bonds a husband

---

[13] MarriageToday.com "Greatest Needs of Men and Women

and wife together in a one-flesh relationship, making marriage unique from any other relationship we can have. You may have intimate conversations with close friends, but that is different from the multifaceted intimacy you will share within your marriage. There is a high correlation between deep intimacy and strong marriage. When intimacy is present, marriages are solid; when it fades, couples revert back into individuals pursuing their own conflicting interests.

The English language falls short of fully describing what God intended to be experienced as intimacy. As an example, Greek has four key words to define love. These words distinguish between erotic love (Eros), brotherly love (Philia), love for mankind (Agape) and the love between parents and children (Storge). English condenses these very different aspects into the single word *love*. It does the same with the concept of intimacy.

"But whoever loves God is known by God" (1 Corinthians 8:3 NLT).

We were created to know God and be known by Him. Just as the words love and intimacy fall short of a full definition, English does not fully represent the word *know* or *known* as was expressed in the original Hebrew. The Hebrew root word for this term is *yada*. This word goes beyond the concept of intellectually understanding something, expanding into the realm of actualization. It's not about grasping an abstract concept but truly embracing and experiencing firsthand someone or something. It's the difference between reading about riding a bike (academic knowledge) and learning to ride by jumping on and pedaling (yada).

You may remember the television sitcom Seinfeld from the 1990s. In many of the episodes, one character would be sharing a story with another. They would provide details up to a point and then would end with "yada, yada, yada." This isn't just a catchy, trendy phrase; it has roots in Jewish culture. The characters were actually saying "I know, I know, I know."

Yada is used over nine hundred times in the Hebrew Bible. In each case it refers to someone having a close, intimate knowledge of someone.

"And Adam knew Eve his wife; and she conceived, and bare Cain, and said, I have gotten a man from the Lord" (Genesis 4:1 KJV).

In this case yada is referring to a procreating, sexual encounter between Adam and Eve. We can all understand and appreciate the experiential, intimate nature of yada in this instance. Interestingly, the same word is used by David.

"Search me and know me" (Psalm 139 NLT).

Here yada is clearly not about a physical interaction but rather a deep and total understanding of David by God. These two examples begin to show the breadth and the richness of the meaning of the word in terms of our intended relationship with God and with our spouse. Yada encompasses both male and female perceptions of intimacy.

Three Aspects of Marital Intimacy

In terms of marriage there are three distinct yet closely related aspects of intimacy. Picture in your mind a three-legged stool. The seat of the stool is the marriage relationship, and each of the legs represent an equal but different aspect of intimacy: spiritual, emotional, and physical. When all three of these legs are solidly in place, the relationship is stable and secure. Remove any of the legs and you will struggle to maintain balance or stability. Ignore any leg and it could erode, leading to unexpected marital collapse.

Let's examine each of the three legs of intimacy in more detail.

Spiritual Intimacy

Before we can have meaningful intimacy with our spouse, we need to have a very real, transparent, intimate relationship with our Creator. Too many Christians have spent their lives reading about and even studying God but fall short of having a yada relationship with him. Achieving this requires us to trust God even when doing so defies logic. It requires us to apply the Word to our lives and transform the way we live. It requires us to move beyond giving God a daily to-do list in our prayer time and to begin interacting by taking the time to listen for His responses. It's about transforming academic knowledge into a yada relationship like David aspired to do.

You can create spiritual intimacy with your spouse by doing things together with and for God. Planning time to pray as a couple, praying for one another, attending church and worshiping together are all good examples of building this intimacy. Over the course of your marriage you will endure some rough spots. It could be the loss of a job, problems with a teen child, unexpected medical bills, or a number of other things. When these occur you will strengthen your relationship when you reach out to God together. External stress is tough on marriage. The divorce rate of couples increases dramatically when these issues cause couples to isolate themselves from one another. Communication suffers when God seems distant. It is important during these seasons to consciously reach out to God together and to rely on His help to protect you and see you through. You will find God may give one of you strength while the other is struggling, and in time the roles switch, allowing you to transform from the comforter to the comforted.

Spiritual intimacy is closely connected to physical intimacy. It may seem wrong to you to include God and sex in the same instance. You may compartmentalize sex into a category isolated from other parts of your relationship. When God created Adam and Eve, they were naked and not ashamed. There was no stigma surrounding sex. It was as natural as conversation or gardening. As soon as Adam and Eve sinned, they recognized their nakedness and hid themselves, not only from God but also from one another. Today we live in a fallen world where the enemy has perverted sex and twisted it into something that, when taken outside of a marriage, is sinful and destructive.

This may sound alarming, but when a married Christian couple makes love, it replicates the type of intimacy we should have with our heavenly Father. When we have sex with our spouse, there is no shame and nothing to hide. In the same instance we are focused on pleasing our spouse and allowing ourselves to be completely vulnerable. Our time spent with God should be similar. God sees us for who we are, flaws and all. He knows our thoughts, our intentions, our dreams, and our fears. Just as we are naked during sex, we should be completely transparent with God, holding nothing back. Interacting with our spouse and God at the same time further cements this area of spiritual intimacy. Over time you will find the compartments established in your life begin to dissolve. Prayer time with your spouse should be incredibly intimate and as natural as making love. Praying before sex will take your experience to a whole new level. Spiritual intimacy begins with God, but it completely spills over into the physical and emotional relationship you have with your spouse.

If you are currently engaged and abstaining from sex until marriage, avoid intense prayer sessions with just the two of you. It is important you share prayer requests with your fiancé. It is equally important you regularly pray for one another. This caution regards the two of you privately engaging in extended prayer together. Think back to the covenant triangle shared in a previous chapter. When you experience heartfelt, transparent, and vulnerable prayer, there is tremendous yada flowing to and from God. That is a wonderful thing. But realize when you have said your final "amen" and look up into your partner's eyes, that same yada will be flowing between the two of you. The temptation to shift between spiritual intimacy and physical intimacy will be very strong. While heartily recommended for married couples, put off this temptation until it can be fully blessed as a part of your marriage covenant. In the meantime, look forward to the day when you can incorporate prayer as a part of your foreplay.

Steps to increase the spiritual intimacy within your marriage:

- Enhance your personal relationship with God.
- Invite the Holy Spirit into your life and into your marriage.
- Pray for your spouse daily in terms of their needs, desires, fears, and frustrations.

- Pray with your spouse on various occasions (even before sex—try it!).
- Strive for transparency with both God and your spouse.
- Serve others in need alongside your spouse.

You will increase the overall intimacy within your marriage when you as a couple increase your yada with God.

Emotional Intimacy

The second type of intimacy is emotional intimacy. While closely related to spiritual intimacy, this is an area focused specifically on nonphysical needs. It's about creating an environment where you share your hearts, become transparent with one another, and support each other in times of stress and need. Emotional intimacy doesn't simply happen. It grows over time as the relationship is nurtured and developed.

Of the three types of intimacy, emotional intimacy is the fuzziest and most challenging to communicate. It is also the most vulnerable and easily damaged. You may know it is lacking but not how to improve it. Emotional intimacy is like a savings account. When you are being kind and attentive to your spouse's needs, you make deposits. When you inadvertently do or say something insensitive, you make withdrawals. The key to satisfaction is to keep a positive balance on the account.

Transparency is critical to emotional intimacy. Transparency is risky in that we fear judgement from others. A common thought is: "If I told someone how I truly felt about something, what would they think of me?" It is against our nature to show vulnerability to others. We have an innate need to seem strong, self-assured, and highly capable. Anything that exposes us otherwise is perceived as weakness. In an effective one-flesh marriage we don't hide our weakness from our spouse. We allow them to supplement and support us in our weakness.

It is important to nurture transparency within your marriage. That will require you to intentionally have intimate conversations. The pressures of life drive couples into informational exchange. Conversations might center around who is going to pick up the dry cleaning or who is going to take Johnny to practice. As schedules get more crowded, it becomes tougher for conversations last longer than a few minutes. Intimate conversations should not be rushed. It is hard for most people to simply blurt out their feelings without some lead-in.

Overcoming this resistance or inability to open up requires God's help (back to spiritual intimacy) but is powerful when it occurs. For this to happen we must have absolute *trust* in our spouse. We must know we won't be judged or ridiculed for being transparent. We must also feel we are top priority in our spouse's life and know they have our back in every situation. It can be horrifying for some people to let their guard down and allow another person to see them for who they are, but this is the key to true emotional intimacy.

It's important to note trust-based, emotional intimacy is incredibly fragile. Of course it can be shattered with betrayal or infidelity, but even a harsh word, a judgmental comment, or a poorly-timed laugh can do damage. I have unintentionally done this a number of times in my own marriage. In some instances it was a matter of oblivion on my part. Tara brought up something she would really like to do, and I responded with an answer like "Why would we do that?" My intention was never to hurt her or violate her trust. Rather, her request caught me cold in the moment, and I couldn't understand the desire or justification for the request. What I intended as curiosity she perceived as judgment. Had I asked her the same question with different words or in a different tone, I might have been fine. Because we are human, emotional intimacy ebbs and flows over time. We must be intentional in keeping it growing and take steps to get it back once we've had a setback.

While we all experience a variety of emotions, the range, depth, and frequency of these vary dramatically from person to person. It can be hard to understand our own emotions in terms of what drives or inflames them, let alone those of our spouse. Stress, hormones, environment, nutrition, even daylight (or lack thereof) can affect how we feel and behave. With the variability in these triggers, it is no wonder our emotions can swing wildly from day to day or even hour to hour.

Of the three types of intimacy, emotional intimacy is the most prone to suffer from misunderstanding. Misunderstanding happens to everybody at some point. Familiar examples may include:

- You say something that offends or hurts your spouse without intending to.
- You say the right thing but in the wrong moment.
- False assumptions are made about a situation, putting you in a bad light.

Here's a great story to illustrate the last point. After about five years of marriage I came home from work one early fall day only to find Tara standing by the sink in the kitchen crying. My immediate response was to rush to her to see what had happened. As I got near she scowled, pushed me away, and cried, "How could you?" I've always been very sensitive and normally can perceive what it is going on in a situation like this very quickly. But in this case I'm sure my face showed pure shock and confusion. As I stared questioningly at her, she reached down and held up a pair of lady's athletic shoes. She waved them in my face and demanded to know whose they were. Having never seen them before I began nervously laughing and explained I had no idea. Of course, my laughter just poured fuel on her already raging fire. "Where did you find them?" I asked. "At the foot of our bed!" she uttered between sobs.

Understanding the context of this story makes it even worse. Tara had been at a work conference for several days and had just gotten back the night before. We caught up with each other for a couple of hours before going to bed. She had the following day off, so I got up the next morning and left for work while she was still sleeping. When she got up later, she walked around to the front of the bed and saw these unfamiliar shoes on our floor. I can't imagine her reaction when she first discovered them, but I can tell you stewing about it all day did not improve her mood or dampen her suspicions.

From her perspective, I had been home alone for several nights. Another woman's shoes appeared at the foot of our bed, and that made me guilty—there could be no rational explanation. From my perspective, I had no idea where these shoes had come from or whose they were. On one hand, she wanted to believe my persistent plea of innocence, but on the other this evidence was pretty compelling. I knew if I was her, I would assume my guilt as well. I had no idea what to say or do to make her believe me.

After staring at each other for about an hour (she wouldn't let me near her to hug her), I went into the other room, still trying to solve this mystery. My mind was racing. I replayed in my memory the entire time Tara had been gone. No females had been to the house in her absence, and there was no break-in at our home. It was as if these shoes had simply materialized out of thin air.

As I was getting ready to sleep on the couch that night, I noticed my gym bag inside the door where I had dropped it when I entered the house earlier. So as not to incur further wrath from Tara, I went over to take my sweaty clothes out and throw them in the laundry. When I picked up the bag, it hit me...I used to play racquetball in the fall through spring months. This was the first day I had played since April. I suddenly remembered getting up that morning and searching for my gym bag that had been stored in the back of our closet for the summer. I hadn't turned on the bedroom light as I wanted to let Tara sleep in. There was some stuff in the bag, but I hadn't paid any attention to what it was. Without giving it any thought, I dumped the contents at the foot of the bed and put my gym clothes inside. Aha!

I went running up to the bedroom, gym bag in hand, and recalled this story for her. As she heard my words, her face turned beet red. She picked up the shoes and suddenly realized whose they were. It turns out Tara had borrowed a friend's shoes and had used my gym bag back in the early summer. She had forgotten to return them, so they stayed there…until I dumped them on the floor in the dark. I dodged a bullet on that one.

We both had a good laugh and some tremendous make-up sex. I wrote the whole thing off as a fun story to share in the future. I came home the next day only to find Tara crying again. "What is it this time?" I asked. She held up a single jeweled earring. "Where was that?" I begged. She went on to tell me it was on the night table beside our bed. Talk about Déjà vu all over again! I knew no more about the earring than I had about the shoes.

Even though Tara had completely forgiven me for the misunderstanding from the day before, finding this jewelry brought back all the feelings of doubt and mistrust she previously held. I felt cursed and had no idea what to say other than to once again plead my innocence. Later that night (a very quiet night I might add), we got a phone call from an older female friend of ours. "Did you happen to find an earring at your house?" she asked.

It turns out she had been at a party at our home the weekend before. Back in the day before everyone had cell phones, she had needed to call her daughter. Because it was loud in the main part of the house, she slipped into our bedroom to use the phone. She would always remove the earring on the side of her face that she held the phone up to so it wouldn't clank on the handset. In this case she forgot to pick it back up. It had simply gone unnoticed until Tara's return.

Trust me. If you ever find yourself in a situation like this, you'd better hope you've built up trust and some emotional intimacy points ahead of time, or you might be staying in a hotel for the night.

Emotional intimacy is always in flux. Your goal should be to grow this intentionally over time. You do this by extending mutual transparency and vulnerability. It is important you exchange intimate conversation with your spouse. Guard and protect trust like a precious gem. Inevitably you'll do or say something insensitive that will set you back. You'll never be perfect at this. Your goal is to endure the setbacks while creating overall growth in the long run.

Specific ways to build emotional intimacy:

- Build trust with your spouse by following through on your promises.
- Provide them with a "judgment-free zone" where they can freely open up and share their thoughts.
- Be transparent and vulnerable with your spouse.
- Share your desires and dreams as well as your fears and insecurities.
- Call your spouse from work just to say "I love you."
- Make sure they know they are the most important person in your life.
- Commit to uninterrupted time together on a regular basis.
- Engage in nonsexual touch and physical interaction.

Physical Intimacy

Hopefully you've saved yourself for marriage. If so, congratulations! If not, keep reading anyway. There are still many ways in which God can bless your marriage. God designed sex, and he designed our bodies in such a way we can receive tremendous physical pleasure when we engage in sex with our spouse. The sexual discovery process is one of the most amazing journeys you can ever undertake. As you explore and learn what is and is not pleasing to both you and your spouse, you find yourselves growing ever closer in your relationship. I once heard an older woman give some very memorable advice to a soon-to-be-married couple. "It's okay to point during sex, and it's okay to laugh. But never do both at the same time!"

We live in a fallen world. While God intended for us to be "naked and unashamed," sin has infiltrated sexuality in a major way. One need only look at the rise of pornography and sexual addictions in our society to see how sex has been distorted into something perverse and forbidden. Just as Eve was tempted in the garden, sex is always just at our fingertips, tempting us into situations outside of God's intent.

If as believers you engage in sex prior to marriage, you experience some level of guilt from your decision. The Holy Spirit convicts you, telling you what you are doing is wrong, but your strong physical desires typically override that "little voice in your head." But that little voice prevents you from fully giving yourself to your partner as God intends for you to do in marriage. Many dating or engaged couples set specific boundaries on what they will and won't do prior to marriage. This is a great thing, but it is important to realize where those boundaries need to be set. God designed our bodies and determined how they function. Passionate kissing, touching, heavy petting, and genital contact were all designed to serve as foreplay. By definition, foreplay is something that happens to prepare a body to engage in sexual intercourse. It is physically unnatural to set a boundary past the point where the body is fully prepared for sex. Stopping there (if in fact you can) will lead to frustration, anger, resentment, and physical pain or discomfort.

God's original design was not for couples to date for years, then be engaged for more years prior to marriage. It is highly unrealistic to think a man and a woman can be together in a growing relationship for that long without crossing the line into sex. The desire for sex is a tremendous incentive for a man to commit to a woman in marriage. When sex is offered prematurely, the incentive disappears. What benefits does he have to look forward to? I think the dating process should be about determining compatibility, confirming desire, and coming to a place of shared dreams. Once those things are determined, it's time to get married.

For some the guilt of others has been passed on to them. They may have been told by their parents that sex is nasty or that good kids don't do certain things. They've been led to believe procreation is the only reason for sex, and having it for mere enjoyment is wrong. I know of others that refer back to their youth pastors who convinced them sex was sinful. At least that is how they perceived the message. If you have been raised in an environment like this, I encourage you to start praying now—prior to your wedding. Pray that God will cleanse your mind of such lies, and He will prepare you mentally, spiritually, and physically to be able to fully accept your spouse in a Godly, sexual manner. Pray you will be open to learn ways to please your spouse and to be willing to engage with them in a manner most pleasing to you as well.

The Bible should be your ultimate guidebook for life, and that includes sex. There should be no guilt associated with married sex. It is also important to note nowhere in scripture does it say things like "Thou shalt only have sex in the missionary position," "You should only have sex with the intent to procreate," or "Your lips should never touch your partner's body anywhere other than their lips." There really is no list of "do's and don'ts" regarding specific sex acts. The only real guidelines are that sex is limited to you and your spouse.

"Marriage should be honored by all, and the marriage bed kept pure, for God will judge the adulterer and all the sexually immoral" (Hebrews 13:4 NLT).

"Drink water from your own well, share your love only with your wife" (Proverbs 5:15 NLT).

Fully explore your sexuality with your spouse once married. There is no reason to rush this process. Ideally this attitude of exploration and discovery will last throughout the course of your marriage. Discuss your likes, dislikes, and preferences together. Don't assume discomfort with any given particular act will last forever. Attitudes and preferences change over time. Keep the lines of communication open to ensure you remain current. Don't withhold your desires but respect your partner at the same time.

I've heard some single people say they couldn't imagine being with just one person for the rest of their lives. They speak of how boring sex would be in that situation. It doesn't have to be that way. I speak from personal experience when I tell you, while the frequency may subside over time, the variety and level of satisfaction does not have to. But it takes effort. If you find yourselves falling into a sexual rut, do something to change things up. Location, clothing, perfumes or colognes, context, timing, positions, and toys are all means of adding variety to a long-term marriage. The one exception to this approach would be pornography. We are told to keep the marriage bed pure. Bringing others into it, even via streaming video, is not acceptable in God's eyes. While watching porn may be arousing, it only causes individuals to lust after others, which clearly is a sin. Keep your sex between the two of you, and God will bless it incredibly.

Sex may be the most obvious form of intimacy in marriage, but it can also be the most volatile. It is rare when a husband and wife share identical sex drives. More often than not, one spouse desires sex more often than the other. The more desiring spouse may feel cheated or neglected if their needs aren't met. The spouse with the lower sex drive may feel put upon if constantly nagged about it. Coming to an agreed upon understanding in this regard is critical to long-term marital success.

Marriage is a covenant relationship that includes God. Sex is intended to be the sign of that covenant and is a critical dimension of healthy married life. God intended for a couple to wait until marriage to engage in sex, removing any guilt or hesitation that occurs when it is experienced prematurely. When a married couple first comes together sexually, it can be an amazing time of passion, exploration, and discovery. Each partner is called to give themselves fully to their spouse and focus on building the relationship. This is not a new concept.

"If a man has recently married, he must not be sent to war or have any other duty laid on him. For one year he is to be free to stay at home and bring happiness to the wife he has married" (Deuteronomy 24:5 NIV).

God understands the importance of starting the marriage off on the right foot. Being available to and for your spouse during the honeymoon phase is critical.

For most couples the sexual drive that exists early in the marriage wanes over time. This is completely natural. There is an old Greek saying: "Put a bean in a jar every time you make love the first year of your marriage. Then take a bean out every time you make love after that. The jar will never be emptied." I don't believe this to be literally true, but I understand the point. As your relationship matures, other issues begin to command your attention, most noticeably the onset of children. Focusing on your career might be another priority cutting into your sex life. Regardless of the distraction, it is important to realize physical intimacy in the form of sex is a critical ingredient throughout the course of marriage. It will change in terms of frequency and athleticism, but it continues to provide a bond essential to a healthy marriage.

No matter what the individual's drive is, we are called to fulfill the needs of our spouse.

> The husband should fulfill his wife's sexual needs and the wife should fulfill her husband's needs. The wife gives authority over her body to her husband, and the husband gives authority over his body to his wife. Do not deprive each other of sexual relations, unless you both agree to refrain from sexual intimacy for a limited time so you can give yourselves more completely to prayer. Afterward, you should come together again so that Satan won't be able to tempt you because of your lack of self-control.
>
> —1 Corinthians 7:3-5 NLT

The Bible clearly tells us it is wrong to deprive your spouse of sex. Each of us is to cede control of our body to our spouse.

It is important to note that nowhere in scripture does it say you should only have sex when…

- …you are feeling on top of your game.
- …you're not too tired.
- …your spouse has earned it.
- …you are really in the mood.

It's no surprise men and women typically have conflicting desires when it comes to physical intimacy. While it is not the case one hundred percent of the time, most men desire more sex while their wives crave more nonsexual touch. This is potential conflict waiting to happen. The husband may have the greatest intentions of satisfying her desire to cuddle, but he may become physically aroused while doing so and wish to take it further. If the wife initiates nonsexual touch, he may confuse the physical contact with foreplay and assume it is leading to sex. In either situation someone is going to end up frustrated and neglected. In time individuals may deny themselves of their true desires to avoid such awkward situations. She may decide to suppress her desire for nonsexual touch in order to avoid leading her husband on. He may stop assuming what leads to sex and simply begin to ask for it directly. Around and around it goes in a nonverbal, passive aggressive power struggle with each partner either wanting to gain control or to avoid blame.

God clearly understood these issues when he instructed us not to withhold our bodies from our spouse and to fulfill their desires. If a man knows he can have sex with his wife most anytime, he has no reluctance in expressing nonsexual touch. If it leads to sex, that's great, but it doesn't have to. He can cuddle on the couch strictly to show affection. It may seem counterintuitive, but when sex isn't something to be negotiated or worked for, the marriage becomes much more relaxed, and frustration decreases for both partners as they can each get what they need.

I've heard many wives complain their husbands want sex all the time, and husbands claim their wives are never in the mood. I think both of these notions are typically overstated and misunderstood. These attitudes place excessive emphasis on sex itself. As I've described, sex is only one aspect of intimacy. Look at this from a perspective of all three forms of intimacy being in play at once. When you find you are in tune with God and directed by the Holy Spirit, you will be far more sensitive to the moods and needs of your partner. Likewise, when your emotional intimacy bank is full, you will find yourself far more willing to engage in sex than if it is empty. A marriage runs on all cylinders when all three aspects of intimacy are in place.

Unhealthy Behaviors

Unfortunately, this is not the way many couples live. They find themselves in a constant, unhealthy power struggle over sex. We see this manifested in a number of ways. From the man's perspective, he may find he has to work to "earn" sex. He may perform a number of actions toward this end, from initiating awkward conversation to buying flowers or even watching a chick flick with his wife. He has probably heard and believes in the crockpot analogy that says if he intentionally warms up his wife all day long, she will be ready for sex that evening.

None of the things he is doing are inherently wrong, but his motives are typically very evident since he only pursues these behaviors when he is striving for sex. From his perspective, doing all of these things will surely put her in the mood and earn sex as a result. On the other hand, knowing her husband only does these things when he wants sex leads the wife to see right through his actions. She feels like she's being manipulated, and that puts out any spark of sexual interest she may have otherwise had. The guy ends up disappointed with a strong feeling of "That didn't work, why even bother?" dissuading him from doing things she would otherwise find desirable. As a result, both partners begin to deny their spouse of desirable activities. Not only is physical intimacy damaged, but spiritual and emotional intimacy suffer as well.

It's not only husbands that manipulate. Wives know the power of sex in a relationship. It's been said many times women have the real control in a marriage since they are the ultimate gatekeepers of sex. I've heard many wives admit they know the minimum of amount of sex their husband requires in order to keep peace in the relationship, but beyond that there may be little interest. Others treat sex as a reward for behaviors or tasks they desire from their husbands, much like training a puppy with a doggy snack. I recall one woman telling me "He finally finished building the bookcase that I had requested for a year. Of course, I gave him sex that night…" This is every bit as offensive as the husband in the first example. While he may accept her offer, at some level he resents having been used in such a manner.

There are several things that bother me about that scenario, but I cringe any time I hear the phrase "gave him sex" or an equivalent phrase. Sex is not something one partner can or should give to the other. Couples in this mode are essentially in a struggle for control. Sex becomes a powerful bargaining chip that can be given or withheld in order to achieve personal gain.

When sex is viewed as a reward or incentive, you create an environment in which there are winners and losers. One partner gets what they want, and the other must concede to some degree. Concessions of this type typically don't come for free. In reality, this approach becomes a destructive game where each partner will seek to even the score over time. These acts of retaliation may surface in seemingly unrelated areas.

- We had sex last night—you can make your own sandwich today.
- You denied me sex last night, so I'm not calling you from work today.
- You never just let me cuddle, so I'm not giving you sex.
- I'm not going to bother taking you out for another nice dinner—it led to nothing.
- We haven't had sex in forever, so I'm going to complain about you to my friends.
- You always have time and energy for the kids but never for me.

The above examples are typically not expressed overtly; they may not even be conscious attitudes. The more the sense of imbalance is felt, the more these behaviors will surface. At some mental level it becomes a "you hurt me, I'm going to hurt you back" situation. If not rectified, it becomes a downward spiral. These behaviors drive a wedge into the relationship, decreasing the likelihood of mutually satisfying sex even further.

The easiest way to deter these unhealthy behaviors is to avoid them from the start of your marriage. These behaviors and attitudes don't typically exist early in a marriage; they creep in over time. Most couples are unaware until they find themselves immersed in them. The key to keeping sex in its proper perspective is very simple but not easy. Are you ready for it?

Surrender your need for control and don't make sex the ultimate goal or reward in your marriage.

In a healthy, shocking marriage sex is not a bargaining chip nor a reward. Just as scripture suggests, it occurs when either partner expresses a desire for it. While there are exceptions, make every attempt to make your default answer "yes" when your partner initiates sex. If a man knows he can usually have sex with his wife when he initiates it, he is far more willing to meet her other needs for intimacy.

While the frequency and intensity of your physical needs will decline over time, they should never fully go away. Sex biologically bonds you to your partner. When sex disappears from a marriage, this bond begins to erode. While you may find sex takes more time and intentionality as you age, you may also find it becomes far more satisfying for both of you as well. As long as you are physically able, it is important to keep sex an active part of your relationship.

Tips for improved physical intimacy:

- Become a servant lover. Put the desires and needs of your spouse ahead of your own.
- Avoid saying "no" whenever possible. This could be in response to a request for cuddling, talking, praying, or making love.
- Understand the ways in which your spouse likes to show and receive love and meet them where they are.

The Three-Legged Intimacy Stool

Strong marriages focus on all three legs of intimacy simultaneously. I worked with a couple in a season of stress. She paid the bills and was working two jobs to help make ends meet. By the time she returned home at night, she was exhausted. As a result their physical intimacy suffered. Though he appreciated her efforts toward covering expenses, he resented the lack of sex in their marriage. He became short with her during many conversations. This unkindness damaged their emotional intimacy. Over time they found it tough to spend much quality time together, and this compromised their joint prayer life, eroding their spiritual intimacy. You can see in this case how these three legs of intimacy are clearly intertwined. When one leg suffers, the others will begin to suffer as well.

Fast forward a couple of months, and the man received an unexpected bonus from work. Without consulting his wife, he went out and purchased a new set of golf clubs. When his wife found out about this, she became furious. How dare he purchase something so frivolous when they were struggling to get by? From his perspective, he was getting no pleasure or satisfaction from the relationship. He hadn't anticipated this bonus, so in his mind the money was his to spend as he pleased. Besides, he *deserved* new clubs.

With no intimacy supporting their relationship, the marriage nearly collapsed. The resulting breakdown in communication prevented either of them from seeing the situation from the other's perspective. Fortunately, they were both strong Christians committed to the relationship. With support from an outside counselor, they began to refocus on their spiritual intimacy. They started by ensuring they were each in daily communication with the Lord through prayer and Bible reading. Then they committed to praying for each other (though at first they both admitted their prayers were directed at changing their partner). Finally, they began to resume praying together.

Once they put their emphasis on regaining spiritual intimacy, God began to change both of their hearts. They began to listen to one another and to support each other in their struggles. This renewed empathy made deposits in their respective emotional intimacy accounts. Once that was reestablished, physical intimacy followed shortly thereafter. Today this couple finds themselves in a shocking marriage where they are very much aware of their intimacy levels. When they see an area start to dip, they intentionally course correct to get things back to a healthy state.

In an intentional, one-flesh marriage it's important to not deny your partner of their needs or desires. Think about your own body for a second. If your leg itches, you scratch it with your hand. If the sun is in your eyes, you shield them with your hand or forearm. If you have a sore ankle, you will naturally limp to take the load off of the hurting leg. In none of these instances is one part of the body trying to convince or persuade another part to assist. It happens without thinking. A need is expressed, and a solution is provided.

I sometimes hear a spouse say something like "I'm just not a touchy-feely person, it's not how I'm wired," Or "I know my wife loves gifts, but I've never been the kind of guy that likes to buy gifts. I don't really value them, and it never occurs to me to buy her something." Once you are married, life is no longer only about you. It's now about seeing to your partner's needs as well as your own. To the previous analogy, a hand doesn't say to the leg, "I don't like to scratch things, so you'll just have to deal with the itch yourself." In a one-flesh marriage you naturally care for your partner and satisfy their needs, be they spiritual, emotional, or physical.

In the early days of marriage your emphasis on pleasing your spouse will come quite easily for both of you. You will walk and hold hands, sit with his arm around her shoulder, cuddle on the couch, and make love on demand. Every part of you will want to please your spouse in every way possible.

Unfortunately, over time couples become less spouse-focused and more self-focused. You've surely heard the phrase "the honeymoon phase," which describes these behaviors in newlywed couples. This decline is not intentional; it naturally occurs over time. You have probably heard of the Golden Rule.

"Do unto others as you would have them do unto you" (Matthew 7:12).

While that's a beautiful and useful teaching from Jesus, I don't think it is fully applicable in marriage. That would imply,

"Here's what I would like. Therefore, I'll offer that to you." I like to talk about the Golden Rule for marriage (my words, not from scripture) "Do unto your spouse, as they would like to be done unto." Following this suggests you learn to meet your spouse's needs where they are, not where you would be if you had those same needs.

Over time it's important to gauge where both spouses are in terms of satisfaction with a given aspect of intimacy. Consider a simple rating on a ten-point scale where *one* is completely unsatisfied and *ten* is completely satisfied. I know of couples where there is minimal sex in the relationship (physical intimacy). The wife is fine with that and would rate her satisfaction as an eight. However, the husband is very disgruntled with this situation and would say he is at a two. In these cases they're in real trouble. The fact that the wife is happy with where she is in no way supersedes the frustration he feels. For other couples it's the emotional intimacy that is out of whack. He doesn't think much about it, but she feels as if he doesn't really care about her feelings or emotional needs. Each of you should periodically talk about where you stand on each of these legs and compare to the other. This is *not* an area for compromise. Using the ten-point scale, if she is an eight and he is a two on physical intimacy, it doesn't mean they should compromise to reach the average of five. In a one-flesh relationship, if he is at a two, then the marriage is at a two on this dimension. When this is discovered, it is important to have a heartfelt discussion to find the root cause of the dissatisfaction and put tangible action plans in place to increase and equalize the score. It doesn't mean they will get to an agreed upon eight quickly, but an agreed upon six is much better than where they started.

Enemies of Intimacy

It is important to proactively focus on all three aspects of intimacy in your marriage. At the same time it is equally important you avoid actions and behaviors that damage intimacy.

Enemy: lack of transparency

All forms of intimacy are based on trust. When you are not open about your feelings or keep things from your spouse, you lack transparency. In a one-flesh relationship you should have no secrets. Without secrets you have no need for personal privacy. It's not that you should never need alone time, but if you need it, explain to your spouse that is the case and how you intend to handle it. Your spouse will intuitively know when something is wrong or when you are struggling with something. If you don't share the cause, you encourage their mind to start imagining what could be going on. Their imagination may be far worse than your reality. You're not saving them stress or grief by keeping problems to yourself. I knew a guy that was unexpectedly laid off from his job. He was ashamed to tell his wife, so he got up every day and left the home as if he was going to work. Some days he would go to interviews, but other days he would sit at a coffee shop for hours to pass the time. It didn't take long for her to intuit something was amiss. Her mind went straight to infidelity, and she immediately wanted to investigate his cell phone and his email. He was reluctant to share these for fear she would see his communication with potential employers. The situation came to a head when she confronted him with her accusations and threatened to leave him. It was only at this point he came clean and confessed. What he perceived as protecting his wife almost destroyed their marriage. Had he been transparent from the beginning, she could have shared in his burden, prayed, and encouraged him every step of the way.

Solution: be an open book with your spouse.

Learn to express your feelings, both positive and negative. Don't try to shield your spouse from bad news. If you have a fear or a setback, bring them alongside. Allow them to carry the burden with you. Share your passwords for every device you own. Let them know they are welcome at any time to check your emails, texts, social media, or any other form of communication. The odds are they will never do so, but knowing they could at any time provides them with a tremendous sense of comfort and relief.

Enemy: lack of communication

You will quickly come to learn, if you haven't already, your spouse is not a mind reader. While they will become more in tune with your unspoken needs as intimacy increases, they will never fully know what it is you desire if you don't share it with them. This can be a huge stumbling block for couples. Women especially want their husbands to know what they want or need without having to tell them. This frustrates the husbands because they feel they can never get it right.

Solution: intentional communication is critical across all three forms of intimacy.

You may be asking your spouse to pray for you or simply to hold you. You may find yourselves in a discussion about sexual preferences and dislikes. No matter the situation communication is important. It is important you set aside time to allow this to happen. Passing conversations in the kitchen regarding your children's logistics does not count. It's not that those issues aren't important. But for many couples this becomes the extent of the communication that occurs. Intentional communication leads to intimacy.

Enemy: boredom in the bedroom

It is perfectly natural for couples to fall into routines. Repetitive habits simplify our lives and keep us from having to think about every little detail as we go about our day. Think about it: if you always hang your car keys on a hook by the door when you get home, you never have to search for them when you're in a hurry to leave. That saves you time and reduces frustration. But beware the temptation to allow routine to creep into your sex life. If you find yourselves only making love in a given position, on a given day, and always in the same location, then you are in a rut. Couples that stay in these ruts for an extended amount of time begin to have sex less frequently because it is not as satisfying as it once was. A major risk with sexual boredom is the enticement of sexual temptation elsewhere, be it through pornography, flirtation or worse—with another person.

Solution: be intentional in not allowing sex to become routine.

Talk to each other openly about desires, preferences, and even fantasies. Go out of your way from time to time to focus on your spouse's sexual needs. Changing your venue is a simple yet effective way to mix things up. Be it making love in a new room in your house or getting away for a night at a local hotel, a new environment stimulates new thinking and new actions. You are limited only by your imagination. Whatever you do, make sure you respect the desires of your spouse. If they are not comfortable with or don't enjoy certain activities, find something you can both participate fully in.

Summary

There is more to intimacy than sex. Intimacy is a multifaceted concept that bonds a couple together. Spiritual, emotional, and physical intimacy together form a three-legged stool that supports a couple in marriage. Each of these legs is interconnected with the others. If any one leg suffers, the stability of the stool (marriage) is in jeopardy. Learn to recognize and meet the needs of your spouse in all three aspects and you will find yourselves in an intimate relationship unlike any other.

Discussion Questions

1. Before you read this chapter, how would you have defined intimacy? Discuss your answers.

2. Discuss Jimmy Evans, listing of the greatest needs of women and men in marriage. Do your needs line up with the list?

3. Discuss the chapter's steps to increase spiritual intimacy within your marriage. Are there any steps you are hesitant to take? Discuss your plans to introduce the steps into your lives.

4. Take some time to read the section entitled "Specific ways to build emotional intimacy."

    - Ask your spouse if you are following through on your promises.
    - Do you have difficulty being transparent and vulnerable? Take some time to consider what the underlying cause(s) may be.
    - Ask if you are creating a "judgment-free zone" where they can freely open up and share their thoughts with you.

5. Read the section on sexual intimacy and discuss:

    - A short definition of *servant lover* was given. Expand on that definition as to how that might look in your marriage.
    - Spouses were encouraged to "avoid saying 'no' whenever possible." Read the description and discuss how to create a culture in your home where this is possible.

CHAPTER 7
SAFEGUARDING YOUR MARRIAGE - *GUARDRAILS AREN'T JUST FOR HIGHWAYS*

Shocking marriages are proactive, not reactive. Proactive couples don't wait for situations to arise before they deal with them. They anticipate potential situations and put guardrails in place. They take regular assessment of the health of the relationship, which includes having an ongoing awareness of their partner's needs, moods, and situations.

Develop a spiritual awareness of what's going on in and around your marriage. Satan doesn't bother with lukewarm Christians doing nothing. He focuses on those trying to advance the kingdom. Take a large step of faith, and spiritual attacks commence. Strive to model a Godly marriage and you might experience attacks as well.

"For our struggle is not against flesh and blood, but against the rulers, against the authorities, against the powers of this dark world and against the spiritual forces of evil in the heavenly realms" (Ephesians 6:12 NIV).

There is resistance to anything beautiful God has designed, including marriage. We live in a fallen world, and there are forces that want to take our focus away from God and allow destructive seeds to be sown, often without our awareness. Sometimes scripture becomes more personal when you make it personal: "For our struggle is not against our spouse…" When you realize conflict in your marriage is generated from spiritual forces, it is easier for you as a couple to align against a common enemy. Satan loves to turn believer against believer, especially in marriage.

"The thief's purpose is to steal and kill and destroy. My purpose is to give them a rich and satisfying life" (John 10:10 NLT).

Christ has a beautiful purpose for us, but the thief (devil) focuses on destroying that intent. While this is true for us as individual believers, God's wonderful plan for marriage has also undergone attack since its inception.

There are a variety of ways the thief will specifically attack marriage. Infidelity, lust, pornography, greed, selfishness, jealousy, and mistrust are only a few of the tools used to tear couples apart. The devil delights when he can destroy Christian marriages as this sends a message to the world that believers are no better or different than anyone else.

The best way to defend against these attacks is to have a high degree of spiritual awareness and to take a proactive stance. In the following sections you will see various areas where marriages are attacked and tangible ways in which you can defend against them.

Make Your Spouse a Top Priority

One of the best ways to safeguard your marriage is to give it high or even top priority. This takes intentionality. It is natural to become complacent over time in a relationship allowing other priorities to creep in. Children, careers, hobbies—even church involvement can sometimes overshadow the importance of marriage. These things don't happen overnight but rather emerge slowly so as to go unnoticed.

Linda said of her husband in a life group meeting that "Life is really busy with work and the kids and all… I know I don't give my husband the attention he deserves, but I know we love each other. He just kind of goes on the back burner; I'll focus on his needs and our needs as a couple later when things settle down."

The reality is that things never settle down. We live in a "fire-fighting" culture where everything is perceived as urgent, and we are continually drawn from emergency to emergency. Without intentionality marriage will never be a priority in your life. As a result your relationship will erode over time due to a lack of focus.

Learn to balance your marriage amongst your other life duties. You work on the things in life to which you give the highest priority. Examples include:

- You put in extra hours at work in order to advance your career. You justify this, thinking this will benefit the family, though in reality it keeps you away from them.
- You are active in a variety of church and civic organizations. You feel social pressure to put in time and effort to ensure their success.
- You spend hours each day caring for, transporting, and supporting your children. They have to be top priority. Everyone tells you they'll be out of the house before you know it.

There is nothing wrong with any of these examples. The only problem is there is typically no similar effort extended toward the marriage relationship. We live in a culture where the squeaky wheel gets the grease. If your spouse is not overtly complaining about a lack of attention, they go unnoticed. Just like Linda, you may have good intentions to get around to them, but there are always pressing distractions keeping you from them.

I've heard it said you can tell a person's priorities in life by looking at their checkbook. That may be true, but in our obsessively busy culture, I think the same could be said by looking at a person's calendar. We schedule the things in life that are the most important to us.

Intentional Investment

Intentional investment is key to keeping a marriage strong and growing over time. Being intentional in your marriage is to consciously give it the top priority it deserves. We typically associate the term investment with finances, but it's bigger than just money. Investment also includes spending time and talent. If being intentional is a mindset, then investment is the action that brings this mindset to life. You cannot say your spouse is your top relational priority if you are unable or unwilling to find time to spend with them.

Matt and Amy were married and had four kids. Matt had the heart of a servant and would help anyone in the church that needed anything, consuming his evenings and weekends with volunteer tasks. Behind the scenes Amy was very unhappy. Things around their own home were broken and in a state of long-term disrepair. She once shared, "He has time for everyone else's problems but our own." While she was proud of her husband's attitude of Christian service, she personally felt neglected and hurt. Not only did Matt not have time to do the projects around the house, but he was too busy for a date night, a getaway weekend, or even a one-on-one conversation with her.

We're told in the Bible we are to give our first fruits to God. That includes treasure, time, and talent—God is to be our top priority. But our spouse should be our second. When they're not near the top of our list, pain and resentment result. In the case above Matt was investing the bulk of his time and talent outside of his marriage, so much so that he was unaware of the pain he was causing Amy.

In contrast, John and Susan were generous with their time, talent, and treasure but kept their marriage a top priority. At a small group meeting one night, the subject of light bulbs came up. Susan shared that burnt out light bulbs were a huge pet peeve for her but went on to say she rarely, if ever, saw one in their house. "John knows I hate seeing them, so he replaces them as soon as he notices them. I never have to ask. I know it sounds funny, but that's one of the many ways I know he loves me…" This couple has their priorities in order.

Money comes into play in a relationship as well as time. Some men like to be showy with their money. They generously pick up the tab at restaurants when dining with friends and buy expensive items at charity auctions. But these same men complain about spending money on their spouses or raise their eyebrows when their wives want to do something for themselves such as get their nails or hair done. The message received by their wives is: "I'll spend money on everyone else without complaint, but if you want something, it's always a problem." Being a low priority is an issue for most spouses, and it should be.

Willingness to invest is important. But it is equally important to be willing to be invested in. If your spouse is making efforts to spend time, money, or talent with you, it is critical to graciously accept these as a loving gift. Flowers are a great example. It's been said a gift of flowers serves no practical purpose whatsoever other than to say "I love you." I've heard of wives telling their husbands they don't want or need flowers —they're a waste of money. These same wives then complain if their husband later buys them a toaster for Christmas because it is so unsentimental. If you criticize every present your spouse makes towards you, they will eventually quit buying you anything.

Investing time works the same way. If a husband suggests having a date night or going away for the weekend and hears "Oh, I couldn't possibly leave the kids," the message he receives is, "Our children have replaced you as the top priority in my life." That is a destructive behavior and puts a wedge in the relationship.

When Jerry was in the corporate world, he led a team with several direct reports. After one particularly challenging stretch involving extensive international travel and time away from families, he was able to provide a bonus to his employees. One team member, Joe, had traveled to India many times over the previous year. He was a solid family guy with four kids at home. Jerry took Joe out to lunch one day and suggested he use some of his bonus money to do something nice for his wife. After kicking around ideas for a while, Jerry suggested he take her on a cruise. Having left her at home with so much responsibility, that would be a great way to reconnect. While this is something Joe had never considered, he liked the idea and decided to surprise his wife with it. He was able to find a relative that would watch the kids for a week, so he bought plane and cruise tickets. Jerry saw Joe the Friday afternoon before he went home to present them to her. He was absolutely beaming with excitement.

When Joe came in on Monday, he looked sullen and dejected. Jerry asked, "What happened?" It turns out his wife rejected the idea completely. She was mortified Joe would consider spending that type of money on something so frivolous and insisted that he return all of the tickets for a refund. She could not justify such a luxury when in her mind they had more pressing priorities. From Joe's perspective, he was not investing in just a vacation. He was investing in his wife and their marriage. An opportunity to move the relationship forward became an issue that caused erosion.

What does intentional investment look like from a practical standpoint? Here are some examples:

- Let your spouse know they are the top priority in your life, not only with words but also with actions. Work around their schedule, attempt to meet their desires, build them up around others, and treat them with a servant's heart.
- Make time to have meaningful conversation with them every day. Go beyond the pressing issues of schedules and kids and see how they're doing personally. Care about their answers.
- Share intimacy regularly with them, both sexually and non-sexually. Kiss them before you leave the house. Give them a pat or a rub as you walk by. Hold their hand in public. Sit together in church. Put the kids beside you, not between you.
- Cuddle.

- Encourage them to envision and fulfill their dreams. Help them in the process.
- Work with them to set visions and goals for your marriage and your family. Check in periodically on these goals to measure your progress. Adjust items in your lifestyle to ensure success.
- Accept their actions and investments in you and your relationship. If they're making an effort to please you, accept it with a gracious heart. Don't question the logistics or the expense. If it's a problem, address it at a different time such as when you are goal setting.
- Identify some projects your spouse would love for you to complete. Surprise them with a completed task.

There are certainly many other proactive forms of intentionality you can make, but these give you an idea of the types of things you should focus on.

Divorce-Proofing Your Marriage

Think about your personal circle of friends, family, and coworkers. How many of them have experienced divorce? Looking at national statistics regarding divorce rates can be overwhelming. I heard one man say, "If one out of every two marriages end in divorce, I guess it's just a role of the dice in terms of my own relationship."

That is not true at all. You are ultimately in control of your relationship, not some ethereal, outside force of randomness, nor the dark forces described in scripture. Going back to the one-flesh relationship analogy of the human body, the hand would never think the foot might simply go its own way, nor would the head think it has grown tired of its legs and no longer needs them. If you are growing in a one-flesh relationship, the concept of divorce should not be an option.

It starts with firm commitment. You will make (or have made) vows to your spouse on your wedding day that probably include the phrase "'til death do us part." That is not a lofty ideal but rather a vow made before God Himself. This is a good promise to recommit to from time to time. Take the word *divorce* out of your vocabulary. Never threaten it nor consider it. Taking that option off the table will force you to work through your issues, whatever they are. Jerry talks more about this in his first book *Rules of Engagement*, where he talks about this being the first rule he and Tara ever created. Simply knowing divorce is not an option drives you to look past a momentary tough time (be it an argument or a longer-term issue) and know you are striving toward a better future. It helps you refocus your energies toward solutions rather than simply assigning blame.

Beyond commitment there is another way to virtually eliminate the possibility of divorce—pray with your spouse. That sounds overly simplistic, but studies have shown this to be effective. Television personality and relationship author Dr. Phil McGraw talks about this in his book *Relationship Rescue*.

> [A]n interesting statistic shared by David McLaughlin in his wonderful series entitled *The Role of the Man (In the Family)* reflects the divorce rate in America is at a minimum one out of two marriages. But the reported divorce rate among couples who pray together is about one in ten thousand. Pretty impressive statistic, even if you reduce it a thousand-fold.

Wow! What a powerful statistic. The problem is that few married Christian couples pray together daily. Going to church together on a Sunday morning is not sufficient to protect your relationship, but spending regular time together in prayer can make it 99.99% likely your marriage will survive.

Once you are married, begin praying with your spouse regularly. This does not need to be a lengthy, highly involved process. Many couples talk about spending five minutes praying together before they head off to work or before they go to sleep at night. "We're just too busy" is not a viable excuse. Think about what is on the line here. As you've read, you find time for the things you prioritize in life, and your marriage should be a top priority.

You may think you don't like to pray out loud or you wouldn't know what to say. You're not speaking to your spouse in these times; you are speaking directly to God alongside your spouse. Pray for blessings, protections, safety, and peace. Pray for the meeting she is facing and is nervous about. Pray for the bad news he has to communicate at the office today. Pray for each other's friends and families. Pray for God's direction in their life and in your relationship. There is no shortage of topics to pray about that involve you both on a very personal level. Praying together brings the Holy Spirit directly into your relationship and further promotes the one-flesh relationship you are seeking. Make this a habit early in your marriage and it will seem natural to do over the life of your relationship.

A Healthy Sex Life Reduces Temptation

You saw in the passage from Ephesians that we are in a battle against spiritual forces of evil that seek to disrupt your marriage. One of the areas the devil will focus on surrounds sex outside of marriage. We see the following advice in Paul's letter to the church in Corinth.

> "Do not deprive each other of sexual relations, unless you both agree to refrain from sexual intimacy for a limited time so you can give yourselves more completely to prayer. Afterward, you should come together again so that Satan won't be able to tempt you because of your lack of self-control."
>
> —1 Corinthians 7:5 NLT

Sex drives should be satisfied but done so exclusively within marriage. When these needs are *not* met, the door is opened for temptation. While seldom a problem for newlyweds, not meeting sexual needs becomes a very real problem for married couples over time, especially once children come into the picture.

For females the onset of children transforms bodies and minds into "mommy mode," a state where the urge to nurture and care for a new life replaces the biological urge to flirt and procreate. This is natural with a newborn, but this phase should not last forever. The problem is that when husbands become fathers, they don't go through the same psychological and physical transformations their wives do. Their sexual desire for their wife does not wane. If as a couple a healthy sexual routine does not return in time, he finds himself in a position of being directly tempted by Satan.

I am not condoning or justifying sexual sin, but I can tell you I have worked with several couples where the husband strayed from his marriage in the three to four years following the birth of his children. The story I hear from them is almost always the same: "We had a great sex life until we had kids. We almost never have sex anymore, and when we do, it feels like she is giving in begrudgingly..." They go on to share how they encountered someone at work or online. Their lack of self-control led them into temptation, and they eventually caved. Some of these marriages were salvaged, but others dissolved in divorce.

Empathy in a marriage is a critical trait, and it must go both ways. Men need to be understanding of their wives during these times, but wives must realize their husband's sexual needs have not dissipated. Be careful not to tee your spouse up for temptation. Open conversations about feelings are critical throughout marriage but especially during these times of likely frustration.

In later years of marriage you will not maintain the frequency or the intensity of sex you experience early on, but it should never go away. Your sex life will erode with lack of attention, so make an effort to keep it meaningful and interesting. If you find it becoming routine or dull, switch things up. Try something different, be it a new position or a new location. If you are bored with sex, blame no one but yourself. Make it a point to keep it interesting over time.

Proactive Steps

- Don't underestimate the importance of sex in your marriage. Make time for it and keep it a priority even when you think you're not really in the mood.
- Make every attempt to satisfy your spouse's sexual needs.
- Talk openly about sex in terms of your desires, likes, and dislikes.

Avoiding Infidelity

"You must not commit adultery" (Exodus 20:14).

Of all the sins we can commit, this one made God's top ten list. Adultery is defined as sexual relations in which at least one participant is married to someone else. The Merriam-Webster dictionary defines infidelity as "the act or fact of having a romantic or sexual relationship with someone other than one's husband, wife, or partner." The word infidelity is virtually synonymous with the word adultery, so the terms are often used interchangeably. The Bible calls out other types of sexual sin throughout the Old and the New Testaments, but only adultery is included in the Ten Commandments. While a tough standard to uphold, we are commanded to stay faithful to our spouse, avoiding sexual sin at all cost.

The lure of sex outside of marriage has been around since the beginning of time. Solomon, the wisest man of all time, wrote the following words in Proverbs:

> For the lips of an immoral woman are as sweet as honey,
> and her mouth is smoother than oil.
> But in the end she is as bitter as poison,
> as dangerous as a double-edged sword.
>
> —Proverbs 5:3-4 NLT

> Drink water from your own well—
> share your love only with your wife.
> Why spill the water of your springs in the streets,
> having sex with just anyone?
> You should reserve it for yourselves.
> Never share it with strangers.
> Let your wife be a fountain of blessing for you.
> Rejoice in the wife of your youth.
> She is a loving deer, a graceful doe.
> Let her breasts satisfy you always.
> May you always be captivated by her love.
> Why be captivated, my son, by an immoral woman,
> or fondle the breasts of a promiscuous woman?
>
> —Proverbs 5:15-20 NLT

Is there anything in this passage that is not as applicable today as it was when it was written over twenty-five hundred years ago? Many marriages are ripped apart because of infidelity. Solomon cautions that you may be tempted but points out the consequences of following through. If you have ever been through a divorce or know someone that has, you know the financial strains that are caused. STDs can gravely injure not only the offending partner but their innocent spouse as well. Infidelity never "just happens." It is always the result of a conscious choice. If, as Solomon suggests, you take a step back and consider the big picture, you will see the inevitable consequences that will arise. He provides a contrasting, proactive attitude you should reflect on and embrace: "…may you rejoice in the wife of your youth." Rejoicing is a choice we make, sometimes with effort but nonetheless a choice. Thank God on a regular basis for your spouse and for the blessing they are. That is an act of obedience that can keep your mind in the proper perspective.

A generation ago infidelity required two people to be in physical contact with one another. With today's technology infidelity can occur virtually over smart phones or webcams.

The above definition defines infidelity as a "romantic or sexual relationship…" Many a physical affair has started with simple online flirtation through social media. Even if a relationship doesn't advance to that point, it is still dangerous and damaging to the marriage. Consider what Jesus said in regard to this.

"You have heard the commandment that says, 'You must not commit adultery.'

But I say, anyone who even looks at a woman with lust has already committed adultery with her in his heart" (Matthew 5:27-28 NLT).

No one is immune from infidelity. No one goes out in search of it, but many fall prey to its lure. We all need to be on guard to the temptations and actions that can lead us down this destructive path.

"If you think you are standing strong, be careful not to fall" (1 Corinthians 10:12).

This passage speaks specifically to those who think they are standing strong by their own power and in their own strength. Such an attitude makes one vulnerable to attack. This is not a modern, cultural phenomena. The Old Testament shows us Samson (the strongest man in the Bible), Solomon (the wisest man in the Bible), and David (the man after God's own heart) all fall prey to sexual sin. Each suffered the consequences as a result. Sexual sin is not inevitable. Admitting you are susceptible to these temptations allows you to build a defense against them.

In a healthy, one-flesh relationship you will come to feel the emotions of your spouse. You'll know when they're anxious, sad, or excited without even exchanging words. You'll laugh when they laugh, and you'll cry when they cry. It's an incredible bond you will share.

Think Ahead

Imagine cheating on your spouse, going home, looking them in the eye, and trying to act as if everything is perfectly fine. You would do everything possible to avoid having any meaningful conversation or even making eye contact. You know they would intuitively sense something is amiss. That would force you into deeper deception to cover your tracks, leading you into physical avoidance. The wedge between you would grow quickly, and the marriage would begin to suffer. If you were to stray, your spouse would suspect it very quickly. Their flesh would feel sinned against.

No one enters into marriage thinking, "If my spouse doesn't fully please me, I'll find someone on the side who will." So why do so many couples end up in this situation? It's fundamentally selfishness and a lack of self-control, but it's also an issue of neglect. Maybe the children consume all the time and energy your spouse has. It's also possible that careers, individual hobbies, or even separate social circles cause the initial divide. Before adultery occurs, the one-flesh relationship is inevitably strained. That's the only possible way one could cheat on their spouse without being sensed or discovered.

When I have counseled couples that have been through infidelity, I've heard men attempt to justify their cheating. "It was meaningless sex. Strictly a physical act, it meant nothing to me…" I'm quick to let them know that is not how it works. If sex were only a physical act, then you could tell any victim of abuse or rape they only need to heal physically, then they'd be fine. That quickly puts things in perspective for them.

Stay proactive and attentive in your marriage. You should find yourselves in a better place in year three than you were in year one (or year thirty compared to year twenty). Provide the effort and nourishment your relationship needs to grow and flourish. You want every bit of your one-flesh relationship to be as healthy as possible.

If you find your level of satisfaction in decline, look at yourself instead of your spouse. You can't change them, but you are in absolute control of your own actions and behavior. Start there, then see what happens.

Proactive Actions

- Surround yourself with Christian friends that will hold you accountable in your actions.
- Take an honest assessment of your marriage periodically. If you both agree you are in a season of decline, make conscious efforts to improve things.
- Identify areas where you can be a better spouse, putting more focus on the needs of your spouse than on yourself.

From a defensive standpoint, the best advice is to radically reduce your risks. Sexual sin is one area in the Bible where we are instructed to avoid rather than confront the enemy. Our physical drives can be so strong that once we find ourselves too far down a given path of temptation, it can be almost impossible to turn around. It's better to not venture near the path at all. So, what are practical ways to avoid the temptation to cheat?

Temptation is different for each person, but if you're honest with yourself, you know where you are susceptible. One man can eat lunch in a Hooters restaurant with no issue. Another will be flooded with thoughts that could tempt him to stray. The same holds true for movies and television. Be honest with yourself and know what lines you shouldn't cross.

Beware the formation of close relationships with people of the opposite sex, specifically in the area of emotional bonding. Most of us work with a variety of people, both men and women. When kept at a professional or superficial social level, this is seldom a problem, but when raw emotion enters the picture, everything can change.

Joe was an executive at a large corporation and had a female assistant he worked very closely with. They regularly joked around and talked about each other's families. One day she came into his office and closed the door. She began crying and telling Joe of serious problems she was having with her husband. Because of their close relationship, Joe listened carefully and empathized with her plight. Over the coming weeks she continued to update Joe on the deterioration of her marriage. She found Joe's attentiveness and sympathy to be very appealing, something she was completely lacking at home. Her thoughts evolved from communication to physical attraction, which Joe found very enticing. He found himself at a fork in the road: pursue the temptation being offered or risk terminating the relationship. One option would bring him near-term pleasure, but the other would protect his marriage.

Vice President Mike Pence was ridiculed by the press when he stated he would not dine alone with a woman that was not his wife. He also said he would not drink alcohol at a party if his wife was not present. From a cultural standpoint these statements seemed outdated and even sexist. From his perspective, he recognized what the beginning of certain paths look like, and he chose not to go near them. He's not alone in these convictions. Many Christian couples share similar beliefs and, for the record, are all happily married.

So, what happens if you find yourself heading down a trail you know you shouldn't be on? If you follow the desires of the flesh, you will get burned. If you use the power of the Holy Spirit living within you, God will provide an escape.

"The temptations in your life are no different from what others experience. And God is faithful. He will not allow the temptation to be more than you can stand. When you are tempted, he will show you a way out so that you can endure" (1 Corinthians 10:13 NLT).

What are the potential outcomes or consequences of a given action or decision you might make? Here's an example. You find yourself in a situation that has become sexually charged much like Joe did. You never meant for it to get to this place, but it did. You know the near-term pleasure being promised is incredibly tempting, and every part of your body is urging you to proceed. In the moment your brain even works to help you rationalize your decision. *You deserve it, right?* If left to your natural self, you will stumble.

Imagine a moment of scenario planning. What happens if and when your spouse finds out (and they will)? Picture the look of shock and hurt on their face. Imagine having to sit down with your children and explain to them why you will be moving out of the house. Imagine having to tell your parents why you're separating. Consider the unplanned expenses associated with lawyer fees and new housing. Who will keep the family dog? You get the idea. It doesn't take but a few moments of this type of thinking to clear your head and lead you to reverse the situation. Every one of these thoughts will come to your mind after you stumble, but at that point it's really too late. Considering them from the beginning could change everything.

Beware the battle taking place in your mind. Remember the verse in Ephesians regarding spiritual warfare and recognize where these voices are coming from. Don't fall for the words of the deceiver. *He loves me. He says he'll leave his wife and marry me. This is what God really intended for me.* Lies! They're all lies. Only three percent of couples involved in an extramarital affair actually get married. Of those that do, seventy-five percent fail in a subsequent divorce. This is a far cry from the deception you were convinced of ahead of time.

Defensive Actions

- Create safeguard rules for yourselves and agree to hold each other accountable. Examples could include:
- I won't go to a lunch or after-hours event alone with one person of the opposite sex.
- I won't have any social media friends that my spouse is unaware of.
- I will share my passwords for my phone and computer with my spouse.
- Know your areas of vulnerability and avoid them whenever possible.
- When faced with temptation think ahead of the inevitable consequences you will face if you fall.

The Destructive Nature of Pornography

Pornography has become a huge issue in our culture. Never before has it been so readily available in such a private manner. A generation ago teen boys might get their hands on a Playboy magazine and hide it under their mattress for secret nighttime browsing. Today any boy with a smart phone or a computer can see images far surpassing what their predecessors could even imagine. Unfortunately, it doesn't stop with teens or even with males. Recent studies show that one third of porn viewers are now women. You would think Christian men would be exempt from this temptation and addiction, but a recent national survey among churches reports that up to sixty-eight percent of Christian men and fifty percent of pastors view pornography regularly.

God designed our brains and our bodies to chemically bond with our partners. When mothers nurse their babies, the skin to skin contact releases a neurochemical called oxytocin, which emotionally bonds Mom to her child. The same thing happens during sex when oxytocin is released, causing us to bond with our partner. I heard one Christian minister encourage couples to intentionally look their spouse in the face when they reached climax. The brain tends to associate and imprint images at this intensely physical moment. He commented that if a man always looks at her breasts at this time, that is the image imprinted. All women have breasts, and they could become the focus of his bond. When he looks his wife in the eyes, only she can become his focus.

Unfortunately, when sexual release occurs while watching pornography, the brain bonds with images on the screen. Making matters worse, when watching pornography, the brain is trained to seek variety during sex. When that becomes the norm, it can be difficult to be aroused with only one partner. Porn is like a drug: over time more and more is desired, and one soon finds themselves in sexual bondage with explicit images on a computer screen. In these instances what God designed to bring two partners together has been misplaced, diminishing the bond between spouses.

Jay and Lisa were a couple in their late twenties going through premarital counseling. They had been living together for about a year. They completed a premarital assessment tool that surfaced strengths and potential issues surrounding their relationship. One of the areas surrounded specific issues each of them struggled with in their own lives. Jay's results came back showing he struggled with both addiction and pornography. He was open in sharing this with Lisa. When asked how she felt about this, Lisa replied, "It's no big deal. I think it's just something guys do." She was aware of this and felt no sense of betrayal or anger. In a subsequent session on intimacy, Lisa expressed frustration that she was always the one having to initiate sex. She rationalized this as her having a stronger sex drive than Jay had. She was also frustrated in the lack of frequency (once per week) but did not make the mental connection that he was satisfying his desires elsewhere. In her mind things would get better once they were married.

Be Transparent with Your Spouse

Satan loves to isolate us in our thoughts and actions. Our natural reaction to dealing with temptation is: "I couldn't share this with anyone…what would they think of me?" I'm a big believer that all Christians should be in an accountability relationship with another same-sex person or a small group of same sex individuals. This relationship needs to be one where a person can share their innermost trials, temptations, and shortcomings. And it needs to be a judgment-free zone where they are not condemned for sharing. Everyone struggles to some degree. When a person opens up and shares their struggles with others, they need to be encouraged and prayed for.

> …God's light came into the world, but people loved the darkness more than the light, for their actions were evil. All who do evil hate the light and refuse to go near it for

fear their sins will be exposed. But those who do what is right come to the light so others can see that they are doing what God wants.

—John 3:19-21 NLT

Every man is tempted. Every man struggles with lust to some degree or another. Shame and guilt drive a man to keep these thoughts to himself, keeping him in the darkness. Sharing these struggles with a trusted confidante shines light on them and helps to drive them away.

I've noticed while men may share these thoughts with another man, they typically will not share them with the most important person in their life: their wife. They fear hurting them or causing undo strife in the marriage. Unfortunately, in most cases they are correct.

Ladies, are you prepared to hear about the intimate struggles your husband is facing? In a high-functioning, one-flesh relationship a couple should be able to share *anything* together. Not sharing does not make it go away. Ignoring it doesn't mean it doesn't exist. Would you rather hear early on about your husband's struggle with lust and need for your prayers or find out later on he has been having an affair behind your back? I'm not saying every struggle with lust leads to physical infidelity. But I am saying that a relationship open enough to divulge such personal issues is one far less likely to fall into continued and deepening darkness.

Let me (Jerry) give you a personal example here. I once went through a brief season where I found myself overcome with lust. At first it was innocent enough—a second glance at a passing woman or minimally suggestive thoughts. I wasn't happy with these thoughts, but it never occurred to me to share them with anyone. As a man I rationalized these as normal. I had no intention to act on any of them. But they didn't stop—instead they increased in frequency and duration. I began to generate incredibly vivid fantasies in my mind involving women I came across. As a Christian I was mortified over the places my mind was going, but I couldn't seem to stop it. Fortunately for me this was before the boom in internet pornography, or I could have gotten sucked right into that. Unfortunately for me these thoughts and desires increased at an alarming rate. One Sunday morning I was sitting beside my wife in church, and I found myself mentally undressing women all around me. That's the point where I knew something was wrong.

We went home after church. As we began to change our clothes, I made the decision to open up to Tara. I confessed everything I was struggling with. In the silent moments that followed, I was not sure what to anticipate from her. Was she going to scream? Was she going to cry? Was she going to hit me? I remembered thinking I'd prefer she hit me instead of crying. I feared her response, but I was in such inner turmoil I couldn't continue on as I was. After she gathered her thoughts, she said the two most impactful words I could have ever imagined. No, they weren't "Get out!" She looked me in the eye and said, "Let's pray." She went on to pray over me and cast out any demonic influences affecting me. She pointed out that I was a man of God, and these evil thoughts had no place in my life or in our marriage. She prayed with boldness and conviction. By the time she said "Amen," I felt like a heavy weight had been lifted from my back as the lustful thoughts and feelings immediately dissipated. I remember distinctly feeling so much love for her in that moment. Whereas I feared judgment and anger, I experienced prayer and healing.

From Tara's perspective, she was surprised when I confronted her with this issue. Her first reaction was one of anger and hurt, but that changed when I asked for help. Because we're invested in our long-term marriage, she was able to look past her immediate feelings and come to my assistance. For the next several months she would ask me from time to time how I was doing in this regard. While she wanted to hold me accountable, part of her motivation in doing this stemmed from her own insecurities and fear that I might relapse.

Summary

The purpose of this chapter was not to frighten you or to cause undue paranoia. Every marriage goes through trials. The key is to put some guardrails in place to help you minimize these trials and protect yourself from falling prey to them. The old saying is true. "An ounce of prevention is worth a pound of cure." Do yourself a favor by being proactive in your relationship, and you will save a lot of stress and grief over the long run of your marriage.

Discussion Questions

1. This chapter gives examples of intentional investment. Discuss with your future spouse which methods appeal to them the most.

2. In the section entitled "Divorce-Proofing your Marriage," you are urged to "take the word *divorce* out of your vocabulary." Have you both affirmed this as a bedrock foundation of your covenant marriage?

3. Do either of you have a family history of choosing the divorce option? Discuss the elements and values that led to the dissolutions of those marriages. Compare them to what you have learned up to this point about a shocking marriage. What intentional commitments to change are you willing to make? Write them down.

4. After you have read the section "Avoiding Infidelity," take some time alone in prayer, carefully rereading the section and asking the Lord to bring to light any weak areas in your own life. Once you have done this, commit to action steps to bring about change. Share them with your fiancé.

CHAPTER 8
EFFECTIVE COMMUNICATION - *YOUR GREATEST TOOL*

Lou's wife loves to welcome friends into her home for dinner. She is a wonderful cook. While she is comfortable serving simple fare, she is passionate about transforming a simple meal into a message of welcome and love by the way it is laid out. A homemade bowl of chili with cornbread can unfold into a feast that will be remembered for years to come not only because it is delicious but via the atmosphere created around the table. A unique set of bowls, sparkling glasses, simple but eye-catching napkins, quality silverware, and a floral display from the garden that welcome the seasons into the home can communicate to the guest: "You matter, you are welcome, you are loved. Sit down, stay, linger." It considers the guest and their needs. It is concerned about what is communicated to them through the experience and what message they walk away with.

Healthy communication in marriage does the same thing. Words that enrich and deepen a covenant marriage are presented with care, lovingly crafted with the hearer's best interests in mind. They can even turn a difficult conversation into a message of welcoming and love by the way those words are laid out.

God's Word says it this way:

"A word fitly spoken is like apples of gold in a setting of silver" (Proverbs 25:11 ESV).

Our words, our communication with others, are the apples of gold, and the way we "present" our words is the setting of silver. We could paraphrase this by saying, "It's not just what you say. It's how you say it."

Do a web search on "reasons for divorce" and you'll find poor communication in the marriage relationship is the top result. The same can be said for Christian marriages.

Often when a married couple comes in for guidance, I will begin teaching on biblical communication as, more often than not, communication is a major factor in their marital struggles.

In order to keep your covenant marriage healthy, you need to keep your communication healthy. This is absolutely crucial since you have promised to love each other for the rest of your lives, cleaving to each other when circumstances are good and when they are challenging. You will have to make decisions regarding finances, raising children, choices of employment, where you will live, where you will worship, who your circle of friends will be, and a thousand other issues, many of them unforeseen. Sadly it is not unusual even for committed Christian couples to struggle in their words to each other. God's Word gives you a formula for effective communication.

"Let no corrupting talk come out of your mouths, but only such as is good for building up, as fits the occasion, that it may give grace to those who hear" (Ephesians 4:29 ESV).

This passage teaches us that our words are one of two things:

- corruptive (putrefying)
- edifying (promoting growth).

Our words can be putrid: promoting decay. We can use words that promote relational decay in our marriage. When we call our spouse names, insult them with cutting or dry sarcasm, or mock them, we are using putrid speech.

Steve and Marilyn had been married a few years when they had their second child. Marilyn gained weight during the pregnancy and was struggling to lose it. Steve's solution to the weight gain was to chide Marilyn, poke fun at her, and make suggestions as to weight loss methods. Such putrid communication did nothing to affirm his unconditional love for his wife. Rather, it crushed her to know that her husband saw her as less than beautiful.

When the goal of your communication is to "win" an argument rather than arrive at a "settings of silver" solution, your speech is corrupt. The same is true if you shower your spouse with profanity or hurtful sarcasm. When you cut off communication in order to punish them or use language intended to dominate through fear and intimidation, you are creating an atmosphere of decay.

Mike and Betsy were a fun couple. They were liked and respected in the church and community. When in the privacy of their own home, Mike would punish Betsy by not speaking to her when they came to a disagreement. Sometimes this would last for days. Betsy would be crushed by the silence, secretly hurting and unable to confide in anyone. Couples who are beginning a life journey together need to make a rock-solid commitment to avoid putrid communication.

Rather than corrupt or putrid communication, a couple committed to a covenant marriage will speak in a way "only as is good for building up." This means edifying your spouse, promoting their Christian growth. Here's the goal: please God with the words you speak to your spouse. The journey to good, edifying speech starts with receiving the free gift of salvation...through Jesus Christ and be filled with God's Spirit (Ephesians 5:18). This gives you the guidance you need to use edifying language.

One pastor said it this way: "The only way we can control our restless tongue is by surrendering it to the power of the Holy Spirit and letting Him enable us to control it." John Eadie stated, "We are one hundred percent dependent on Him and at the same time one hundred percent responsible to act even though we can do so only by His power."

One year I (Lou) decided to really work on my lawn. I bought more weed and feed than was perhaps allowed by law, and little by little I used every grain of fertilizer. As spring arrived, I was amazed at how beautiful the grass looked. A thick, lush, emerald green meadow surrounded our home, and our bare toes loved it. I invested a lot of time on that lawn, and the benefits were clearly visible. Edifying words have a similar "redemptive effect" on your spouse. It sets them free to grow and thrive as you free them from corrupting words. In many cases you come into your marriages with a heart full of weeds because of the putrid communication you have been exposed to. Edifying communication can bring health and growth to a marriage.

What kind of words? The edifying words we use to speak to our spouse need to be filled with gratitude for them (Philippians 1:3), love, humility, gentleness, and patience (Ephesians 4:2). When a spouse communicates with words intended to promote their growth, it makes it possible to gently point out any blind spots they may have. One pastor said, "Before you point out a flaw, you have to love me." This is certainly true in a covenant marriage.

Tony married Gwen, a lively, beautiful, outgoing woman. She would light up a room merely by entering. The secret of the relationship was that Gwen had baggage. She was raised by abusive parents who would "shred" Gwen with their words. Gwen picked up this trait and brought it into her marriage, redirecting the impacts of the abuse on Tony. Over the years Tony gently and patiently worked with Gwen as she battled her family legacy, using transformative words that had a redemptive effect on her life.

In order for your words to "build up your spouse," you need to be tuned in enough to understand what their real needs are. They are not the same as yours. If you don't understand their needs, even words spoken in love can wound. You think you really know your spouse well before you marry them, but as the years go by, you will come to understand that you have only scratched the surface of understanding. Over time your spouse will grow and change. It is a labor of love to be a student of their evolving needs and an act of humility to dedicate yourself to meeting those needs.

Simon's wife Elizabeth lost her father to cancer. He was a good, decent man who loved his daughter deeply. Her loss took her to a place of sadness that Simon had never seen in her. Simon realized his wife's needs had changed for a season. He needed to add a large measure of patience and understanding as she worked through the grieving process.

As another example. Hudson's wife came to him excitedly with a dream of starting a business of her own. He showed enthusiasm for her vision and affirmed the skills he saw in her that would make this endeavor a success. As a team they worked out a budget, location, company name, and other details.

In each of these cases the husband looked behind the emotion to discover what troubled, saddened, or gladdened his spouse. Once that was understood, they could support their wives in a manner most befitting to their needs.

"That it may give grace to those who hear."

AT Robertson writes that grace (known as *charis* in Greek) has "a variety of applied meanings. They all come from the notion of sweetness, charm, loveliness, joy, delight, like words of grace."

"Everyone spoke well of him [Jesus] and was amazed the gracious words that came from his lips" (Luke 4:22 NLT).

A covenant marriage with God as an honored member is going to be a marriage filled with gracious words. A husband and wife will extend grace to each other just as the grace of God has been extended to them. This will, of course, manifest itself in gracious communication, especially in challenging situations. That kind of gracious communication is truly "shocking"!

Matt comes home from work to find Sarah exhausted with frayed nerves from a stressful day with the children, most of the tasks for the day undone. Matt, who has had a long hard day as well, graciously says to Sarah, "Please let me serve you," and proceeds to take over the family's needs while Sarah rests. He prepares a meal, gets the children settled, and performs a quick clean up. As they sit at the table for their evening meal, Matt leads the family in a prayer of thanks for the meal but says a special thanks for Sarah.

> "As husbands and wives our words must be an example of the grace of God."
>
> —R. Kent Hughes

In your quest to communicate graciously, may I suggest three "big picture" ideas?

Listen Gracefully

"Spouting off before listening to the facts is both shameful and foolish" (Proverbs 18:13 NLT).

How does one "graciously" listen?

Listen swiftly: James tell us to be "swift to hear," giving us the idea that you respond to your spouse's need to be heard with a sense of urgency. Their need for communication with you immediately supersedes everything but the most pressing of tasks on your list. The TV is shut off, the book is closed, and the phone is set face down and on silent. If necessary, your appointment is rescheduled.

You not only agree to hear, but you do it enthusiastically, coming alongside your loved one. Your tone of voice communicates concern, your eye contact as you face them communicates undivided attention. You are listening graciously.

Listening graciously is challenging. This is especially true when the other person is upset with you or criticizes you unfairly. In many cases they are responding to other pressures or fears, and you may be the safest target.

On a lazy Sunday afternoon Lou and Sara decided to sit in their back yard and enjoy the weather. They brought both the dog and cat with them. They were having good conversation when, to their dismay, their neighbor's dogs, a boxer and a husky, escaped their own house and entered their backyard. The dogs were driven off but not before they attacked the cat and bit Sara's hand. After taking care of Sara, Lou went to care for the cat. Speaking kind, comforting words to Dewey, Lou assumed the role of "cat whisperer" and picked him up to hold him (bad idea, I know). Dewey responded to Lou's kindness by biting him on the side of his face. He had been wounded, and he struck out in fear. People can be like that. Wounded people tend to wound others, and in our married relationships there are times where we will respond to our external crises by attacking the one who loves us the most: our spouses.

When this happens, it is important to lovingly search for the root of their angst. Are they approaching a calendar date that marks a watershed event in their life? Is there conflict at work that they struggle to leave at work? Is there a medical or emotional issue behind their actions? Of course, when they are truly upset with you, listening with the goal of resolving is an art that needs to be refined and developed over a lifetime.

Listening swiftly must also include picking up nonverbal clues. This is part of listening as well because much of communication is nonverbal. It can include facial expressions, but it may also be expressed via gestures, tone of voice, eye contact, and more.

Lou led a couple in premarital counseling, and it was clear the two were responding to him differently. The bride had known Lou for twenty-five years and had been in his youth group as a teen. The relationship with her was warm and friendly, but it was the first time he had met the groom. As they began to talk and lay out the plan for counseling, it became clear the groom was on edge and defensive. Body language, lack of eye contact, and tone of voice made it clear something was wrong. When he was asked about his obvious "edginess," the groom admitted he was defensive because his previous wife had left him, and while trying to keep his marriage together, the last pastor had flippantly said to the groom, "Your marriage is done, get over it." This caused the groom tremendous anger and emotional pain. No wonder he was defensive! Time put the groom at ease, and they enjoyed a joyful wedding and are now happily married.

Picking up nonverbal clues is part of listening graciously. A loving spouse is going to be a student of their spouse with the goal of meeting their needs.

A question to probe nonverbal clues can include:

"It's clear that you're really upset, sad, troubled, etc. Help me to understand what is wrong. I'd like to help if I can."

Clarify Graciously

As we saw in Proverbs 18:13, not listening well is a "shameful thing," but there are times when one needs to ask clarifying questions. Rather than interrupt and cause frustration, wait until your spouse pauses and consider using statements that are gracious but also help you to understand the issues at hand. Clarifying questions can include:

- "May I repeat what you have said to make sure I understood you?"
- "I don't want to put words in your mouth, but may I paraphrase what you said?"
- "Back up a bit. What did you mean when you said…?"
- "What you are saying is important to me. What do you most want me to understand?"

Speaking Gracefully

There is one whose rash words are like sword thrusts, but the tongue of the wise brings healing (Proverbs 12:18 ESV).

We've all seen battle scenes that portray swords or bayonets. When portrayed accurately, they can be disturbing and hard to watch. The anger of the attacker, the helplessness and pain of the wounded, and the aggressive violation of the human body can leave the audience unsettled. As much as we'd like it to be different, we aren't the Marvel character "Wolverine," who could be stabbed hundreds of times, then heal in a matter of minutes and go on to smoke a cigar and play a game of pool. Life doesn't work that way.

When Proverbs tells us that rash words are like "sword thrusts," it gives us a word picture that is intended to be violent, damaging, and disturbing. We can't shrug off rash words as if they were nothing. You may still be bleeding emotionally from words that were said to you when you were a child. It is also true that the closer the bond with one who wounded you, the worse the pain of the words.

Conversely, we've also seen the amazing work that can be done by a skilled medical team in surgery with multiple instruments. Life and death situations can become a "life" situation because of the work of a scalpel. Likewise, incredible scarring damage done to a face can be all but eliminated by the gentle work of a scalpel and the healing of time.

When Proverbs tells us that "the tongue of the wise brings healing," we get a picture of the words of our mouth being an instrument for healing, not hurting—building up, not putrefying. Healing words can take away wounding words from the past. Even when we have to tell our spouse a difficult thing, our words can act as a scalpel; the goal is healing.

"Wounds from a sincere friend are better than many kisses from an enemy" (Proverbs 27:6).

A good guide for gauging healing words has been called "traffic signal" communication. It helps a couple gauge the health of words. We've all driven up to a traffic signal and seen the light burn a bright green as we are driving through. We can proceed in relative confidence that we can cross the intersection in safety. A yellow light doesn't mean we should slam the brakes on our car, but we should use caution in crossing, carefully gauging the safety of our actions. A red light tells us in no uncertain terms to stop the car and wait for the light to turn green. How does "traffic signal" communication work?

Green Light:

When in "green light" mode the couple is facing one challenge or another. Together, using building words and rejecting putrefying words, they identify the problem and attack it.

Scott and Traci budgeted an amount for the monthly needs of their household. Traci would withdraw the amount from the bank account and manage it for that pay period. On one occasion Scott noted that Traci had withdrawn a significantly larger amount. When Scott came home, he approached Traci and said, "You must have had some significant expenses to prompt you to withdraw more money than you and I had budgeted. Can we talk about that?" Traci sighed in relief and shared how she had been hit by larger than expected expenses. She was trying her best but found herself falling behind on taking care of household needs. Together they sat down and worked out a plan to adjust the budget. No criticism, no accusation—only green light communication. Green light will filter words through these three questions:

- Is it true?
- Is it necessary?
- Is it kind?

Yellow Light:

As you approach an intersection, you see the light has gone from green to yellow. In less than a second questions fly through your mind: *Do I stop? Do I drive through? What is the point of no return"?* Whatever the question you ask, you can sum it up in one word: caution. In our communication with our spouse, "yellow light" communication occurs when a couple is facing one challenge or another. Instead of using building words in their communication, they use putrefying words. Instead of identifying a problem and attacking it, they verbally attack their spouse. They are attacking the person and not the problem. You can sum this situation in one word: caution.

The Bible is full of stories that include yellow light communication.

- Moses' wife called him a "a bridegroom of blood" when Moses had neglected the rite of circumcision for his son and she had to act.
- Michal, David's wife, called his actions shameless and vulgar when he danced before the Lord.
- Jacob mocked his wife's emotional pain as she battled with infertility by asking her, "Am I God?"

It is sometimes tempting to use this same attack method when dealing with our spouse.

Tyler was an Architect who had a thriving practice. He and his wife, Candace, were raising three children and were active in their local church. But it was clear to many they were struggling in their communication with each other. It was common for Candace to speak derisively or sarcastically of Tyler when they disagreed on an issue. It was a common thing to see one rolling their eyes when the other spoke.

Phrases like "You *always* forget," "You *never* do what I ask," or "That's just like you, you are so…" are all examples of yellow light communication, made up of attacking words. Do you find yourself in this mode of communication? It's time to sit down and commit yourself to a new approach to communicating.

Red Light:

You are approaching an intersection and the traffic light is red. It's time to apply the brakes. It's time to stop. Ignoring the red light at an intersection is an invitation to disaster. In our communication with our spouse, "red light" communication occurs when a couple is facing one challenge or another. Instead of using building words in their communication, they use putrefying words. Instead of identifying a problem and attacking the problem, they verbally attack the covenant relationship they have with their spouse, attacking the relationship and not the problem. You can sum this situation in two words: critical condition.

"I wish I had never married you."
"I'd be happier single."
"I want to take the kids and go far away from you."

Roger and Gina had been married for years. Gina became frustrated at times with Roger and would make negative comparisons between Roger and men at work. Gina eventually expressed those comparisons to her husband. Sadly, it wasn't long before Gina acted on those comparisons.

When a couple finds themselves in this situation, it is highly recommended that they seek counseling with their pastor or a Christian counselor who embraces the biblical teaching of a covenant marriage.

Resolving Gracefully

"Hatred stirs up strife, but love covers all offenses" (Proverbs 10:12).

It is a fact of life that some couples look at communication with their spouse as a competition.

- The goal isn't to resolve; the goal is to win.
- The motive isn't love; the motive is pride.

As a result resolving issues with your spouse is an exercise in probing for weaknesses and inconsistencies in their arguments to achieve a decisive victory. Who can yell the loudest? Who gets the last word in? We bring up the past and rub their noses in it. When we do this, both parties lose and lose big. God's Word has a better way:

> "Be kind to each other, tenderhearted, forgiving one another, just as God through Christ has forgiven you" (Ephesians 4:32).

In short, just as Jesus tenderly, compassionately forgives us, we should resolve the differences with our spouse in the same way. I heard a wise man once say, "You will never have to forgive your spouse more than Jesus Christ has already forgiven you."

It's Not Just Your Words

An oft quoted study conducted by Dr. Albert Mehrabian in 1967 found that fifty-five percent of all communication is expressed through body language, thirty-eight percent through vocal signals, and only seven percent through words themselves. Since that time there has been a lot of debate over the specific basis of his experiments and the exactness of the findings. Even if he was off by a large margin, we can agree that communication involves much more than simple word choice.

Take for example the word "baby." If your partner calls you this using a soft voice and a certain twinkle in their eye, you will hear it as a term of affection. The same word spoken with a sharper tone and a sneer would be received as a derogatory remark implying that you need to grow up. Clearly the same spoken word could lead you to have very different reactions.

While we do need to be very cognizant of our word choice, we also need to be aware of our inflection and our body language. Urgency, sincerity, sarcasm, skepticism, and lack of concern are all examples of feelings communicated through tone and body language. If you want to prove this to yourself, try watching a familiar television sitcom with the volume turned off. You will be amazed that you can follow the bulk of the plot just by watching the characters interact without hearing a single word.

Early in their marriage, Jerry and Tara would get into heated debates. When frustrated, Jerry would slow down his pace and overenunciate each word he spoke. Tara would get very upset and insist he stop yelling at her. Jerry would defend himself and point out he had not increased his volume at all. While he was literally correct, that's not how she was hearing it. The reality is that if Tara felt she was feeling yelled at, she was in fact being yelled at. Over time Jerry learned how to express himself without the perception of shouting.

Just as with the example above, you may not be aware of how you are perceived in a given conversation. It is important to communicate what you are perceiving when in a conversation with your spouse. Just as tone can send an unintended message, body language can be misinterpreted as well.

Jerry is a big picture person who is never short of ideas. Often times he works through an idea as he is speaking. If he is excited about the idea, it is important to him to fully express his thought so it is not lost. A sudden disruption can derail his thinking and cause him to lose his train of thought completely. Knowing this about himself, he would hold up his index finger if someone were to interrupt him in these moments. In his mind he was simply asking the other person to "hold their thought for a moment" until he could fully express his idea. Tara on the other hand saw this as a demeaning gesture, implying that Jerry did not appreciate her point of view and wanted her to be quiet. As soon as he would raise his finger, she would become hurt and angry. When he finished his thought, he would wait for her comment, but it wouldn't come. Because she was upset, she was unwilling to share her point of view. It took years for this to come to light. One day after Jerry put up his "hold please" sign, Tara blew up and told him how much she hated when he did that. Jerry was quite shocked and replied with a "Did what?" response. She mimicked his gesture and told him how it belittled her when he held it up to her. He explained his intent and his reasoning. They were both surprised to hear the other's perspective. Today Jerry tries not to hold up a finger, and Tara attempts to let him fully express a thought, knowing he will be all ears after he's finished.

If your spouse does something that bothers you, it is important to share that with them. Just as in the above example, it could be that no disrespect is intended, but it is being perceived in that way. Letting that eat at you over time is not healthy for you or the relationship. It is very likely that it is simply a misunderstanding or a difference in interpretation. With knowledge comes change and understanding.

Lou and Sara were raised in very different environments culturally, economically, religiously, socially, and more. Communicating well with each other has been a challenge at times. Lou would say one thing, and Sara would hear something different. Likewise, Sara would communicate, and Lou would read into her motives from his perspective of someone raised in a different culture. They both loved the Lord and loved each other, but at times it felt like they were reading life from two different scripts.

A wonderful tool that they have added to their communication toolbox comes from author Brené Brown. In her new book about resilience, *Rising Strong*[14], Brown shares the phrase "the story I'm making up."

In an interview with Business Insider, she says, "Basically, you're telling the other person your reading of the situation — and simultaneously admitting that you know it can't be one hundred percent accurate."

Take David and Sophia for an example. Sophia delights in preparing lunch for both of them as they go to their separate jobs. She packs each item with care, including a sandwich, fruit, cheese stick, and a midday snack, topped off with a love note written on his napkin. She lovingly plans the lunches as she grocery shops, looking for items she thinks he will enjoy. David appreciates the care she puts into each lunch and looks forward to reading her note, carefully putting in on his desk after lunch as an encouragement for the rest of the day. He enjoys Sophia's creativity in this workweek task. There is only one thing that bothers him: she will prepare his sandwich with the heel of the bread at the beginning of the loaf and the end. Sophia, David notices, never gets the heel. David never mentions it to her but accepts that Sofia at times can be a bit selfish, reserving the softer parts of the bread for herself.

---

[14]

One day as they are planning for an upcoming weekend getaway, they begin to get frustrated with each other. Sophia wants to take the train downtown, shop, and go to a nice restaurant. David wants to take a day trip to the State Park, hike, pack a picnic, and bring the dog. Sophia hasn't been shopping in a while and presents her plan to David, this time a little more passionately. At this point David says "For once, I'd like to do something I want to do. The story I'm making up is that we always do what you want, you always get what you want—just like the lunches you make me! You always give me the heel of the bread, always keeping the softer parts for yourself." Sophia quietly waited for David to finish and then said, "When I was growing up, my mom would make sandwiches for the family, a lot like I do. She'd carefully plan each part so our lunches were an adventure, the envy of our friends in the school cafeteria. One of the treasures of our lunch was to see who got the heel. In my family it was the best part of lunch, and whoever got it was the lucky one!" David and Sophia took the train downtown that weekend.

Lou and Sara have found this tool to be helpful. Not only does it clarify their personal point of view, but it gives their spouse a peek into their heart. This gives them a chance to understand and even minister to their loved one. When growing up, Lou's family was very private. Family meals were rare, and siblings rarely communicated what went on in their personal lives. Conversely, Sara's family regularly sat for family dinners, and plenty was shared. There were few if any topics off limits. When they first started dating, this difference took a lot of work and patience to work through. Using linguistic a tool like "the story I'm making up" can gently open doors and bring healthy communication into a marriage. It would have been very helpful from the start of their relationship.

To make the path to good communication even smoother, it is important to start with the premise of believing the best in each other. Assuming your spouse has the best of intentions as you communicate with each other, believing they are on your side for your good, will help you to overcome a lot of frustration or misunderstanding. Adopting this philosophy will allow you to pause a conversation if or when you hear something unexpectedly upsetting. "What you just told me is very insensitive and hurt my feelings," might be met with an "I'm so sorry, what I was intending to say was…" When you assume the best about your spouse, you give them a chance to make things right. If you don't have such trust, you read bad things into situations where they were never intended.

Here is a critical point when considering marriage: if a fiancé does not have a history of trust in their spouse where long term, tangible integrity has been proven by their actions time and again, they cannot depend on "believe the best" communication and should seriously question whether they should marry.

Joe and Donna were engaged to be married, and while Donna cared for Joe deeply, there were numerous flags about Joe's character. Rumors of womanizing and dishonesty seemed to surround him, and people who knew him in high school and college warned Donna he was not worthy of her trust. As their engagement proceeded, she began to doubt his trustworthiness because of subtle things he would do, deceptions that would be discovered and justified. She could not believe the best in him but married him anyway. They were divorced in a year.

Contrast this story to Drew and Mandy. Mandy was in Lou's youth group when she was in middle school. She was a young lady who had all the characteristics of a woman who would make a wonderful life partner. She truly lived out her faith. After a time Lou accepted a call from a ministry at a church hundreds of miles away and served there for eleven years. It was here he met Drew, a young man who had all the characteristics of a man who would make a wonderful life partner. He worked with the youth and served on the worship team, selflessly giving of his time, talent, and treasures. When Lou returned to the city where he served as a youth pastor, he was delighted to find Amanda attending the church where he was now serving as a pastor. Drew and Mandy…he had watched both of them over the years and saw their godly actions and attitude, so with a mischievous smile on his face he "friend suggested" them on Facebook. They talked on the phone for hours and shared their faith journeys, and it wasn't long before they learned to "believe the best" in each other. These two, who were hundreds of miles away from each other, became man and wife and are faithfully serving the Lord today.

Summary

Effective communication is critical in a marriage. But it takes effort and intentionality. Too many couples take communication for granted, and it suffers as a result. When it is good, it builds up trust and intimacy. When communication is bad, it creates mistrust and hard feelings. Learn to use your words wisely, building up your spouse. But also be aware that your tone and body language also communicate a tremendous amount of information. Be careful of assumptions. Take the time to ask for clarification if something said seems amiss. Let your spouse know what it is you are "hearing" from your conversations and allow them an opportunity to clarify if they've been misunderstood. Applying these principles to your marriage will establish a good and healthy relationship.

Discussion Questions:

1. Ask each other, "Do I use words that are putrid?"
2. Share with each other a time when their words edified you.
3. Discuss what words you can use that "give grace" to them.
4. Ask, "Are there things I do or don't do that make you feel like I am not listening graciously?"
5. Discuss red light, green light, and yellow light communication with each other. Have you gone to yellow

at times? Red? What phrases need to be purged? What needs to happen to get you to green again?

Note: if you are going to "red" in your communication, it is strongly suggested you see a good counselor to work on communication.

6. Ask, "How do you perceive my body language when we are in discussion? My tone? Are there things I do that I'm unaware of that affect you (positively or negatively)?"

AFTERWORD

Congratulations! You have just invested time and effort into your future. Hopefully you have learned some things about each other, had some interesting conversations and have put plans in place for moving forward. You probably have a wedding coming up, if so, we pray that it will truly be a wonderful and blessed event. But as exciting as that is, remember that it is not the finish line, but rather the beginning of a life-long journey together.

Creating and maintaining a "Shocking Marriage" is not complex, but it does require focus and attention over time. Remember, the things in life that you focus on will get better. The things in life that get ignored erode. At some point in your relationship the newness will wear off. You will begin to feel comfortable with each other. Comfort is a double-edged sword. While it is wonderful to be totally at ease with each other, be careful not to become complacent. Invest in your marriage in terms of time, money and talent. Keep each other a top priority, even when the world seems to need every bit of your attention. And most importantly, keep God as your focus, inviting Him into your decisions, direction and calling.

Closing Prayer

Lord, we pray for the couple that has just completed this book together. We pray that You will unite them under Your covenant, lead them as they become one flesh and bless their ongoing relationship. Grant them your peace, flexibility, and understanding for the course of their life-long marriage. We pray Your blessings upon them. In Jesus name – Amen

ABOUT THE AUTHORS

Jerry McColgin

Much more than just a counselor who doles out truth, Jerry McColgin is an involved friend who winsomely speaks truth into a couple's life by gently shepherding them into a place where godly counsel, soaked in grace with a dash of humor, is given. He is a sought-out advisor by many couples regardless of their stage in life. Through his writing, podcasting, coaching and speaking he encourages couples to have the type of incredible and unique relationship that God intends them to have.

Jerry has been writing a popular blog "Shocking Marriage" for over a decade. He is a member of the Christian Marriage Bloggers Association (CMBA). His first book, *Rules of Engagement* (Christian Faith Publishing, 2018) has been met with critical acclaim and has been used both by individuals and by small groups around the country.

Prior to becoming a marriage minister, he lived life as a corporate executive, an entrepreneur and a business consultant. He is the founder of Shocking Marriage Ministries, a group founded on fighting complacency and creating lasting intimacy in marriages. Jerry has been married to his beautiful wife Tara for almost forty years. They have four children and (as of this writing) seven grandchildren.

Lou Rodriguez

"To Know Lou is to Love Lou" is a common sentiment expressed by the hundreds of couples that Lou has counseled both from a premarital perspective as well as those in crisis. His heartfelt advice and non-ceasing humor provide him with a unique perspective that has enabled couples to enjoy a lifetime of marital happiness. He has been in Christian ministry for 35 years as an educator, youth pastor, associate pastor and senior pastor

Lou is a gifted public speaker and has spoken at churches throughout the country on a variety of topics including marriage and relationships. He has hosted retreats and marriage workshops. He has been the guest on popular podcasts bringing his perspectives on effective communication within marriage. Lou is a graduate of Dallas Theological Seminary. He has been married to his bride Sara for 36 years. They have 4 children and six grandchildren.

www.ingramcontent.com/pod-product-compliance
Lightning Source LLC
LaVergne TN
LVHW011826060526
838200LV00053B/3920